BE THE BANK

HOW TO PUT YOUR MONEY TO WORK IN REAL ESTATE

BY
STEVEN VANCAUWENBERGH
with Walter B. Jenkins

BE THE
BANK

HOW TO PUT YOUR MONEY TO WORK IN REAL ESTATE

International Standard Book Number: 978-0-9859805-2-8

First printing 2023

Printed in the United States of America

Published by Teflon Publishing,
800 NE 63rd Street, Suite 200, Oklahoma City, OK 73105

Library of Congress Cataloging-in-Publication Data
is available from the publisher

To my wife: I can't express the support you have bestowed on me.

To the investor: Never give up and ask for the money.

To the private moneylender: Be the Bank and say yes to yourself.

CONTENTS

INTRODUCTION

I was born into poverty. I spent my youth being raised by a single mom who worked three jobs to provide the basic necessities, food, and shelter. I started working at the age of eleven to help provide and enjoy some of the small things all the other families had.

The work I've done over the years has been backbreaking, stressful, and intense. Coming from poverty, hard work was the only way I knew how to move forward. I envisioned a life that allowed my mom to enjoy her days instead of constantly worrying about bills, a life that allowed us to live in a house with two bedrooms instead of a cramped one-bedroom apartment that required one of us to sleep on the couch. The only way I could envision to get there was by working my butt off.

I didn't have the advantage of watching my father work and manage his money. He bailed on us when I was two, leaving my mom as the sole caregiver for my older brother and me. We lived in a series of crappy apartments in unsafe neighborhoods, often with little or no furniture. My dreams of a better life were the few things I had that couldn't be repossessed.

I carried that thought with me throughout my life. With the work ethic instilled in me by my mom, I succeeded in the business of real estate. It wasn't easy by any stretch of the imagination. I worked hard seven days a week, 365 days a year. I was always on, pounding the pavement to find deals. I scratched and scraped and took some risks that paid off in the long run.

When I was married and started having children, I discovered that making money the hard way would have to become second priority. I have a wife and three beautiful children who want to spend time with me, and I want to spend time with them.

I started looking for easier ways to make money. A trusted friend suggested using the money I had been stockpiling in a Roth IRA to do private lending. In the beginning, I was a little leery of this suggestion, but I started doing research. What I found changed my life.

Private money is close to my heart, but I got into it by accident. When I met my wife, I had been self-employed for a long time. I was hustling as a disc jockey before I got into real estate. My money was tied up in rental properties, and that's how I planned my retirement. My father-in-law didn't understand that, and he wanted to feel more secure about his daughter's future. I wasn't worried about that because I was building a real estate empire that would pay for a retirement that most people only dream of. However, to keep the peace with my wife's family, I started an IRA and put some money into it.

When I learned about private money lending, that IRA allowed me to jump in. After spending months researching self-directed and checkbook IRAs, I took the plunge and moved my Roth IRA to a self-directed IRA, which allowed me to use the funds in the account to purchase and own real estate. My Roth IRA was annually earning anywhere from negative one percent to five percent. Each year I would see a little gain or a little loss, depending on the market. It wasn't a good use of my savings. At the time, I wouldn't have noticed much of a difference if I had taken the money out of the account and buried it in the backyard.

Being a private moneylender has changed all that. I never see less than an eight percent increase on my funds. Understand that eight percent is the low end. I normally make from ten to twelve percent on private money loans. The really special thing about making money this way is there is virtually no work involved. After years of crawling under houses, ripping out drywall, and hoping my contractor didn't rip me off, is the "no work" concept was a relief.

The rewards that come with private lending are far greater than just the return on your investments. It gives you the opportunity to help up-and-coming entrepreneurs get their futures started.

Now that I've been at this a while, I constantly receive a multitude of inquiries about private money. People want to know how they can become private lenders, how they can find private lenders to fund them, and how to raise funds to use for lending, among other things.

When someone asks me about private money lending, I get so excited about explaining it that I often miss major details about the multitude of opportunities that are created by being a private moneylender. Writing this book will help me lay out the ins and outs for people who are interested in doing what I've done.

Ultimately, I want the wild world of business to be a win-win for the smallest investor, as well as the professional who is willing to deploy $500,000 to achieve a no-money-down deal for an investor like me.

The goal of this book is to educate potential private lenders about how private money lending works. I have never seen a book written like this one—a book that introduces the concept and benefits of private lending to individuals seeking a decent return on their money. I also want my readers to know it's possible to play a role as a passive investor.

STORY TIME: THE SAVVY INVESTOR

"All successful people ... are big dreamers. They imagine what their future could be, ideal in every respect, and then they work every day toward their distant vision, that goal or purpose."

–BRIAN TRACY

If you look at my early life, there is no reason you would have expected me to achieve any success, but I kept grinding and didn't stop. I had a dream and didn't let go.

I want to tell you a little story about how real estate investors can help average people get better returns. It's called, "The Savvy Investor."

Once upon a time, there was an individual who had money to invest, so he went to the bank. The banker said, "We would love to take your money. We will pay half of one percent." The man thought that was too little.

The man took his money to the stockbroker. The stockbroker said, "I would love to take your money. If the market goes up, you could make money. If the market goes down, you could lose money."

The man didn't like hearing that. It was too risky. "What can I do?" he asked.

Then, one fine day, the man went to see a real estate investor and asked, "What can you do for me?"

"We believe in safe and secure investments that have predictable returns for people. Does that sound like something that could be good for you?"

The man said, "Yes, but how does it work?"

"Well, when we buy, we buy at deep discounts. We then renovate the properties and sell them at good and fair prices. This allows us to make a substantial profit, and we work with people just like you to finance the transaction, so we are able to share some of the profits in the form of interest. Mr. Investor, there are five different things we do that ensure we protect our investors. Remember, I not only said profitable, but safe.

“We provide title insurance.

“We provide homeowner insurance or a hazard policy that names you, Mr. Lender, on the policy.

“We also have a low loan-to-value. What does that mean? Loan-to-value, sometimes called LTV, is the difference between the loan amount and what the property can be sold for. We keep that margin over twenty percent. We would never borrow more than eighty percent on any particular project. That would include both the purchase price and the repairs. If these two add up to more than eighty percent, we will not complete the transaction.

“The fourth thing we provide is a mortgage. This pledges the house as collateral, and the mortgage is recorded in public records showing you as the lender. We also provide you, the lender, with what is called a note, or an IOU.

“Last but not least, we don't just shake hands and call it a deal. We finalize each closing at a title company where everything is out in the open. We document the transaction with a HUD or closing statement, which you probably used when you bought your own home. The statement shows where money comes from and where it goes, so everyone has a clear picture.

“So, Mr. Lender, we buy the property, we renovate it, and we sell it. At that time, we repay the loan and any remaining interest that is due. What do you think?"

"Sounds good. How do I get started?"

"That's simple. We will schedule a time to sit down and talk about exactly how we can best work together. Then we will discuss how much cash you'd like to put to work, how long you'd like it to work, what kind of transactions might work best for you, and the date you'd like to begin."

Everyone lived happily ever after.

MAKE YOUR MONEY WORK FOR YOU

Here's the deal. You have some money. You worked hard for it, and you're not sure what to do with it. Maybe you have it invested in stocks or bonds, or maybe it's in a shoebox tucked under your bed because you don't want it sitting in a bank. You might be holding on to it while you try to figure out if cryptocurrency is a long-term strategy or just a fad that is going to crash and cost a lot of people a lot of money.

You want to find some way to make that money work for you. After all, it took a lot of time and effort to put that cash in your pocket. You want to make sure it repays the favor by bringing in more money for you.

You have heard of—or thought about—investing in real estate. You know your friends and family are making a bunch of money doing it, but it doesn't sound like a good fit for you. The idea of pounding the pavement and looking for properties to rehab and rent or flip sounds like a pain in the butt. Maybe the idea of getting a call at 2:30 in the morning to unclog a toilet is even less appealing than the notion of tracking down deadbeat tenants the first day of each month.

You know there is money to be made in real estate, but you want to find something more passive than investing in properties. Perhaps you are already building your real estate empire and want to find another revenue stream.

In the 1800s, a lot of people from across the United States packed up and moved west. They were looking to build their fortunes by finding gold. Some of them did; in fact, some of them made tons of cash. However, many of them didn't. Would you like to know who made out like bandits, though no one seems to remember them? They are the people who sold those prospectors their equipment. If you are in the middle of a gold rush, you want to be the person selling shovels and pans.

Right now, it seems as if everyone has gotten into the real estate game. Many of them are making piles of cash and living lives others only dream about.

Guess who is cashing in on this and making tons of money? Banks are—or, more specifically, moneylenders are.

Most real estate deals aren't done with cash. A few are, but the reality is that most are done with borrowed money. There are a lot of reasons investors borrow money to make deals happen, and they borrow a lot of it.

Investors usually turn to banks, like the stores that sold shovels and pans during the California gold rush, but they look for money wherever they can find it. This creates a ton of opportunities for people like you—people who have some cash socked away.

I know this from experience. When I was working to build my empire, I needed cash. When you see a smoking hot deal on a property that will fit into your portfolio and make you serious money for years to come, you need to be able to write a check before another investor comes along and seals the deal. Investors need quick and reliable access to cash in order to grow. If you're not growing, you're dying, and nobody wants to be in that position.

However, there are problems with borrowing money from banks, problems every investor wants to avoid. If you can offer solutions to these problems, you will have a stream of people lining up, each one of them representing an opportunity for you to make money.

One of the problems in dealing with banks is that there is so much paperwork involved. It seems as though you have to document every cent you have made since your parents started giving you an allowance. Banks don't want to take any risks or hear about any surprises. If you have hiccups in your background, banks will pull away faster than you can blink. Of course, most of us have some dents in the fenders of our pasts, like getting divorced or being laid off from a job.

There comes a time when every investor has used every penny in the line of credit his bank gave him. I think that's a good thing. If you are borrowing a ton of cash, it means you are getting deals done and making money, and that's the name of the game. If you aren't borrowing money, you probably aren't growing, and nobody wants that.

The point is that every investor needs access to cash, and they are willing to pay for it. That creates an opportunity for you to make a lot of money in real estate without having to search all over the county for properties to buy, a way that is secured by real property.

Sound good?

That's what we'll be talking about in this book—how you can use your money to become a private lender and about helping investors who need access to money. It's a great way for you and investors to build wealth together. You can make as much money as you want by becoming a private lender and helping other investors build their empires.

Before we go any further, I want you to know I wouldn't have been able to start building my empire without a private moneylender.

When I got into real estate, I had no idea what private money was. I didn't even know what an asset or a liability was. I was introduced to these terms in a book called *Rich Dad Poor Dad*. I didn't understand what they really meant. I only knew that an asset puts money in your pocket, and a liability takes money out of your pocket.

However, I was so motivated to change my future and to stop living in poverty that I was willing to do whatever it took. I figured I would buy assets just like the book said to do. I learned about real estate auctions and went to one. The house I was interested in was the second house for sale. I was ready when the auctioneer announced it was up for bidding. "This is the way you build wealth," I told myself, as I tried to stay calm. "You buy assets."

The bidding started at $10,000, quickly went to $11,000, and had reached $13,000 when I decided to raise my hand. When my hand was halfway up, I thought, *What am I doing? I don't know anything about this house or real estate.* But I cleared my head. *How can I go wrong? This house costs less than a lot of cars, and I want to be a real estate investor.*

Moments later, the gavel came down, and I won the auction with a bid of $14,500. I was ecstatic. I'd set a goal and achieved it by purchasing my first investment property. I knew I was on my way to financial independence.

Once the excitement subsided, reality slapped me between the eyes. I realized I was going to have to pay for the house. How would I find the money for it? The auction required me to put down five percent of the purchase price when the auction was over. So, I wrote a check for $725, even though I had no money in the bank. I told myself, "I have twenty-four hours to come up with $725. I can do that." I smiled, walked out the door, and headed for my house.

The next day I pawned everything I could to get my hands on $725. I deposited the money in my account and was thrilled to know the check would clear. This was twenty years ago, long before Venmo was created, and people would often write checks that wouldn't clear, knowing it would take days for the check to hit the bank. It gave me a few days to hustle and get the cash together to make sure the check cleared.

However, I wasn't out of the woods yet. I had thirty days to come up with $13,775. *That shouldn't be a problem. I could go buy a car that costs more than that,* I thought.

Banks were quick to let me know it wasn't going to be easy. I couldn't get a loan anywhere. The main problem was that I was self-employed, which was a really taboo in 1999. On top of that, I was a mobile disc jockey. I played at parties and weddings and had built a pretty good business, but most bankers had no idea what a DJ was or if it was even a profession.

I spent a week calling every bank willing to listen to me, and none of them would give me a loan because I had no proof of income. I worked for myself and couldn't bring in a stack of pay stubs, though I was making money.

I was desperate and saw my dream slipping away. With no other options left, I turned to the one person who might be able to help me. I called my mom in California and explained I had just bought a house at an auction and needed her help to get a loan. She said she would check into a few things and get back with me.

In a few days, she called back with great news. She procured a loan from Bank of America. They couldn't believe she was buying a home that cost only $14,500. I would have the money in time for closing.

When I got off the phone with my mom, I felt a huge sense of relief and accomplishment. I was on my way.

That was the start of my real estate investing. I had a limited education, no money, and virtually no one who could help me, but I was still able to buy a home that I ended up selling for a profit.

This all happened because my mom believed in me and stepped up to help, and I did whatever it took to make it happen. That is one of the reasons I am such a believer in private money lending.

THE WHY

There are a lot of reasons to be a private moneylender. The most important one is that it is a great opportunity to make money. Let's be honest. That's the only reason you would open a book like this. A lot of books talk about that. The difference is that this one delivers.

Let's take a more detailed look at why private lending might be a great opportunity for you.

1. Private lending gives you better returns than other investment opportunities.

When investors need cash, they typically need it quickly. If they wanted to wait weeks or months, fill out a bunch of paperwork, and keep their fingers crossed while they wait for a group of loan officers to vote on whether or not they are credit worthy, they would use a traditional bank. However, investors need access to cash that is quick, easy to get, and ready to access. That's why they need private lenders.

Investors are willing to pay for the privilege of borrowing your money, and they are willing to pay a lot more than what they would pay a bank. Obviously, there are a lot of factors involved, but using your money to lend to real estate investors can earn you an annual return of eight to ten percent. Cha-ching! It's not a bad way to let your cash grow, and it's also passive. You don't have to do a lot of work, and it's virtually risk-free, but we will talk more about that later.

CASE STUDY
Chad Harris

The owner of Arrival Homes, Chad Harris, was working overseas in the ministry and had experience raising money for the ministry. When his fourth child was born, he had health issues which meant Chad and his family needed to stay in the states for his care.

With no income, Chad decided to go into real estate full-time to provide for his family. He wanted to buy-and-hold rentals for long-term wealth, and he shared his vision with many people. He raised money from private lenders to purchase and rehab properties in and around Trotwood, Ohio, and then refinanced with another lender. The deal worked, and he kept repeating the process.

He built a portfolio of fifty-five units before getting his first bank loan. His lenders were happy with the consistent returns knowing their investments were secured by real estate. To this day, he continues to use private money to build his portfolio.

One of the sweet deals he cashed in on was his deal from direct mail to high equity absentee owners. The seller had inherited the house and lived out of state. The seller viewed the house as a headache they needed to get rid of. He purchased the property for $26,000 in cash. The rehab was fairly cosmetic and cost $9,000.

A private lender lent him $40,000 to purchase the property and rehab it as a first mortgage. The ARV was $70,000, and the private lender was confident lending the full amount at closing knowing the loan-to-value was below sixty percent.

The terms of the loan were six percent interest with no payments for two years, at which time all principal and interest were due.

He spent $35,000 on the purchase and rehab and kept the remaining $5,000. After the rehab, he rented the house for $875 per month. He earned a cash flow of $725 per month because he didn't have a payment.

When his term with the private moneylender was up, he refinanced the house with a $59,500 loan. The lender was paid interest and principal in full and was ready to lend on another deal.

Chad had already completed many deals by the time he had done this particular one, so the financing was not difficult. The lender had previously done deals with Chad and has done more deals with him since.

One of the issues the investor faced during this deal was contractor turnover, so the rehab took longer than it should have. He kept trying new contractors and was able to complete the project.

Chad is a huge fan of no-money-down deals. The lender was glad to have an investment to diversify his portfolio that earned him a solid return while being secured by real estate, which means no risk. The seller was thrilled to have a headache out of his life, and the tenant was excited to have a nice home to rent.

His lender earned six percent on his money for two years, which came to $4,800, while being a completely passive investor. Chad made $5,000 at purchase and $17,400 in rent over two years. Another plus was receiving over $14,000 cash when they refinanced to invest in their next deal. Chad still owns the property, and it continues to perform well.

Crunch the Numbers:

Purchase price:	$26,000
Renovation cost:	$9,000
Total investment:	$35,000
Private money loan:	$40,000
Interest rate:	6 percent
Term:	2 years
Lender profit:	$4,800
Lender return:	6 percent
Investor profit:	$22,400
Investor ROI:	Infinite

2. Being a private moneylender is easier than flipping houses or being a landlord.

I love the real estate game. I've been in it for over twenty years, and I can't imagine doing anything else. It's allowed me to live a lifestyle most people only dream of. I get to spend as much time with my family as I want, and I don't have to be tied to an office five days a week. I do what I want, when I want, and I wouldn't trade that for anything.

I didn't just fall out of bed and start having this life. I've done everything in the real estate industry to build a financial empire that gives me freedom and opportunities. Flipping houses? Been there. Landlord? Done that. There's a lot of money to be made doing those things, and they are how a lot of us get our start.

However, these things have their drawbacks. If you want to flip houses or be a landlord, you first have to go find houses. When you are starting out, that probably means you will be the one who is looking for houses to buy. You have to search online, get in your car and drive around the neighborhoods where the deals are, and you have to connect with people in your circle to find deals that fit within your portfolio.

Once you finally find a deal that works for you, there is even more work to be done. You have to get the property ready for tenants to rent or for you to sell, and that may mean putting on a new roof, stripping the walls down to the studs and redoing them, or fixing electrical or plumbing issues, and that's assuming everything goes well. You might get an early Christmas present when the seller hands the keys over to you. Maybe you go into your new house for the first time and discover that the previous tenants messed up the plumbing. Maybe bees set up a hive in the crawlspace after the inspection was done, and you have a full-blown honey operation over the master bathroom. The point is, there will always be things that need to be taken care of when you buy property. It's how the game is played. When you are starting out, those are things you will be doing by yourself, and they take a lot of time, energy, and sweat.

You also have to find buyers or tenants, and that takes even more time and energy. If you want to grow your business and turn it into an empire that gives you your dream life, you will start the process all over again and look for another house to flip or to turn into a rental property.

Don't get me wrong. I love flipping houses and owning rental properties. They are great ways to build a business and create an incredible future for you and your family, but they take a lot of time and effort, and if you have some money there are easier ways to be a part of the real estate game.

Being a private moneylender is about as passive as you can get. You don't have to crawl under houses to see if the plumbing is in good shape, you don't have to demo any walls, and you don't have to chase down deadbeat tenants to get paid. It's not free money, but it's close.

CASE STUDY
Kenny LeBlanc

Kenny LeBlanc is a medical professional in his mid-forties. He grew up in a rural town in Oklahoma and was raised by two college-educated parents. From a young age, the goal of getting an education and a "good job" was instilled in him. His parents were frugal and relied heavily on certificates of deposit and savings accounts for retirement. Investing in real estate and other "risky" investments were never really discussed.

Kenny has been actively involved in buying real estate since the spring of 2018. However, he has been exposed to construction all of his life, and he converted a personal house into a rental when he was in his mid-twenties.

His first private money deal was a loan to a friend who purchased two condos off market to rehab and sell on the MLS. The loan was for a maximum of six months with six months of guaranteed interest, even if the loan was paid off early, which is also known as a prepayment penalty. Each loan was for nine percent interest.

They set up two separate loans, one for each condo, which were valued at $41,000 each.

Because it was his first experience with a private loan, Kenny felt that "not knowing what to do" was his biggest challenge. The fear was easy to resolve. The custodian of his self-directed IRA told him what forms were needed and how to fill them out. With that, he was in business as a private moneylender.

One of the things that made this deal appealing was that Kenny liked the idea of six months of guaranteed interest, and that turned out to be a good thing. One condo was rehabbed, listed, and sold within three months, and the second was sold in the fifth month of the loan.

Private money lending was a success for Kenny. He made $3,690 with his idle cash in less than six months without having to do any work. The seller made money and had the ease of selling the property off market without Realtor fees, selling the condos for $65,000 and $66,000, respectively.

CASE STUDY
Jeff Cichocki

Jeff became a very conservative investor after he took a few lumps. While his two youngest kids were still at home, he got involved (possibly addicted) to real estate investing. It's been a fun and challenging ride for him. He lives in Green Bay, Wisconsin, and has been actively investing for seventeen years, mostly doing private or hard money lending. It started out as a hobby to help his friends and eventually grew into a fairly substantial business. Currently, he closes more than 200 loans per year.

A borrower came to him with a nice property in a great part of town. The purchase price, rehab numbers, and ARV all seemed solid. It looked like a great deal by all normal standards, and he thought he would crush it.

The property was used as collateral, and the borrower personally guaranteed the loan. There were two big challenges on the deal. The first was that the house only had 698 square feet. Small houses usually sell very slowly, and this can make it hard to recoup an investment. The second issue was that the borrower had a ton of wholesaling experience but had zero rehab experience.

To overcome these challenges, they spent some extra time doing two things. The first thing was to triple check the ARV, rehab estimates, and the number of days the house had been on the market. Once they confirmed the property would sell quickly once it was rehabbed, they reached into their borrower pool and found someone they trusted. They helped them partner up on the deal with the borrower and made sure it was someone experienced who would be a good mentor for the borrower.

Jeff's company motto is "Good People, Good Business." Jeff loved this deal because he was able to help someone with no experience to gain the knowledge and skills they needed to make it a great property. Because of the partnership, Jeff was able to help two borrowers. It's about more than just the numbers to Jeff—he loves helping people succeed.

The deal worked out exactly as Jeff had hoped it would. The borrower got the rehab done ahead of schedule, sold the property for more than asking price, and Jeff was paid back on time. Because the borrower crushed it, he came back for another loan, and Jeff made even more money.

Crunch the Numbers:

After-repair value (ARV):	$145,000
Rehab cost:	$29,000
Origination fee:	$4,340 (four points)
Closing costs:	$1,340
Private money loan:	$108,500
Term:	6 months
Interest rate:	13 percent

3. Being a private moneylender is safe because you are in control of your money, and you can diversify by spreading it across as many projects as you want.

We all know people who invest in the stock market. There's nothing wrong with that. Given the right circumstances, it can be a decent way to invest. However, I don't think the returns are as good as they are in real estate, and a lot of people agree with me.

There are a few problems, other than the rate of return, that come along with buying and selling stocks. First, when you invest in the stock market, you don't really own anything. At best, you own a tiny percentage of a company. If you are lucky, that company will grow, or at least not lose too much value when the next bust happens. There *will* be another bust or scandal; it's just a matter of when or where.

When you invest in a company, you also put all your faith in the CEO or board of directors. Suppose you take the money Uncle Fester left you in his will and buy 1,000 shares of Bob's

Hot Tubs, Inc. You've done your due diligence, and it looks like a sweet deal. Everything you've read makes it look like the stock is ready to take off.

Three days after you buy the stock, you login and look at your portfolio. The value of Bob's Hot Tubs has taken a nosedive. News broke in the middle of the night that the CEO, Bob, hasn't just been selling hot tubs. He has been "inviting" every female member of the staff to join him in a hot tub for "personal training." Then someone released old emails from Bob that show he made some racist comments.

You may think this is far-fetched, but do a little research and see how many companies have had to do damage control because one person in the company turned out to be a scumbag. Then try to figure out how much money the shareholders in those companies lost. I don't know about you, but I work hard for my money, and I don't want to lose any of it because someone else can't keep his mouth shut or his pants zipped.

Other people invest in mutual funds (which own stock in many different companies that have proven to make money over time) or invest in different companies. This seems safer because it spreads out the money and the risk over multiple companies.

Mutual funds sound great, but who is in control of making the choices? Is it you, or is it someone living in a yacht purchased from the fees you and all the other investors paid? How can you be sure the fund has the best stocks and is being managed the way that is best for you?

You can't. You have no control over where your money goes once you send it to your money manager or put it in a mutual fund.

You also have no control over the fees that you will be charged to invest in a mutual fund or the fees that you will have to pay if you want to move your money into a better investment.

Here's how it works with private lending. You, and only you, have complete control over where your money goes. When an investor comes to you and asks you to sign a check and give it to him, *you* get to decide yes or no. *You* can review his proposal, look at the property, see how much equity the deal has to secure your money, and *make your own decision*. You don't have to rely on anyone else's judgment, and the best part is you don't have to make someone else rich by giving them a share of the profits.

Another benefit is you can lend money on as many—or as few—properties as you want. You don't have to put all your eggs in one basket. You can invest in different kinds of properties. If you have a loan on a residential property that is smoking hot and is making you a lot of cash, but you are worried that the residential market is about to cool off, you can lend to an apartment buyer or someone who wants commercial property.

If you decide you don't want to lend any more, you can invest however you want once your current deals are done. There won't be any penalties for pulling your money out and putting it back under the sofa.

You also have control over the kind of investors you work with. Not every investor is wanting to rehab to rent or sell. Other investors need cash to build or develop properties, and there are also commercial investors. The point is that there are a lot of different pies, and you get to choose which ones you put your fingers into.

Being a private moneylender gives you the freedom and control to decide where your money goes and how it works for you. It's also one of the most passive ways to make money, so passive you will practically be making money in your sleep.

CASE STUDY
CJ Estel

CJ Estel started investing in real estate when he was about thirty-five. When he was young and dumb (as he calls it), he decided to start an information technology (IT) consulting business. He was handy in many areas of technology, and, despite being in IT, he is actually personable, and he's capable of carrying on conversations and making sales, which doesn't often come easy for tech nerds.

During college, as he ran his business, CJ had delusions of grandeur but had no idea how to get to where he wanted to be. He had no idea how money worked and no idea how business worked, but he knew he didn't want to work for "the Man." Ultimately, what he had created was a lifestyle business with hundreds of bosses and clients to please. This business had no recurring revenue built into it and was not a business he could ever leave. It was really just a job working for himself, and he didn't even know it.

In 2008, some of his largest clients ran into financial difficulties, which ran downhill to him like a giant sewer line that had backed up and covered his dreams with a mountain of crap. With his lack of business knowledge, he held on to employees and failing concepts far longer than he should have. By 2010, he was on the verge of bankruptcy. He knew the choices he had made in his life were ultimately what landed him where he was—an able-bodied individual who was working more than 100 hours a week to keep his head above water with nothing but piles of debt to show for it.

CJ started working with a business coach who helped him dissect and analyze his business. He taught CJ the difference between being a business operator and a business owner. The coach stressed that as an owner you need to work *on* your business and not *in* your business. He helped CJ learn the value of recurring revenue and multiple streams of income. With all of this newfound knowledge, CJ came to the realization that nearly all of what he had built in his company was based on a foundation of sand and that it would require serious change to transform it into the viable business he had always dreamed of.

CJ decided to close up shop and get a "real job." As he communicated his plans to his customers and attempted to refer them to other companies in the area, a few of them did their best to keep him from leaving. That created an opportunity, and he was able to raise his rates by about 600 percent. In hindsight, this meant he probably hadn't been charging enough when his business was open. The increased rates meant he could retain a few customers as a side gig. Ultimately, without having to carry the staff and office overhead costs, he ended up making more working a few hours a week than what he had made with multiple employees. He excelled at his day job, and it felt as if he had all the time in the world. He had been so accustomed to working more than eighty hours a week that working a flat forty hours per week, plus a few hours of consulting on the side, was a breeze.

Over the following eight years, he worked for a few different startup companies. He continued to study business and had the luxury of talking to successful business owners on a regular basis. He saw two of the companies he had worked for or consulted with get to a point when they were bought out for hundreds of millions of dollars, and a third one was bought out for over a billion dollars.

He saw the success that he had helped others generate, and his desire to run his own business had never been stronger. He looked at his finances. He had eliminated nearly all of his personal debt with the exception of his primary residence. He had impeccable credit, and he was back on track with "where he should be," according to financial experts, regarding what he had set aside for retirement. He came to the realization that he didn't want to do what everyone else was doing. He didn't want to retire at sixty-five. He wanted to set himself up for success and start making decisions that would allow him to invest in himself and his family. He wanted to be able to enjoy time with his kids during their impressionable years.

He talked with his wife, and they decided to use some funds from their home equity line of credit (HELOC) and contributions from his Roth IRA to use as down payments on a couple of rental properties. After the first couple of properties, he got the itch to keep growing. He found a new mentor who focused specifically on real estate and who was able to accelerate CJ's growth beyond his wildest dreams. He introduced CJ to the concept of private moneylenders and dispelled the myth that you need to have money to invest in real estate. While it is necessary to have your own funds and cash reserves, being able to leverage outside funding can open up many new doors.

With his mentor at his side, CJ was able to identify profitable deals. With relatively decent accuracy, he learned to identify repair costs and understood how to determine what a good maximum allowable offer (MAO) should be. If you do it right, you should be able to buy the property, rehab the property, and pull *all* of your purchase costs, holding costs, and rehab costs back out using a traditional bank finance. In many instances, you can still end up with leftover money in your pocket from the refinance. Or you can look to sell the property for larger cash injections up front. CJ's strategy has been to hold the real estate for better long-term gains.

Over the next three years, with the knowledge he had gained and having continued mentorship, CJ was able to safely work with investors and give them great returns on their money. He was able to do this while having their money secured by a physical asset (the property) that will be worth far more than the money they lent him. He has developed great relationships with the investors who lend him private money, and they are able to time their refinances with other deals. This helps them roll their funds into new deals and continue to get great returns. CJ and his wife now own twenty-one properties comprising over 140 units. He has been able to replace the income from his day job and is looking forward to financial freedom and more time with his family as he continues to grow his real estate holdings.

His best private money deal was in Lancaster, Ohio. The property had gone to sheriff's auction for a tax lien sale. Tax sales are unique sales in that they generally take priority over all other liens against the property, and after a tax lien is satisfied or sold via auction, the remaining liens are dismissed.

This property was 4.65 acres of industrial land less than a mile from the local hospital. Years prior, it was home to Anchor Hocking Glass Corporation, which was the largest employer in the county. They had bought the property in 1992 for $220,000. Years later, Anchor Hocking did some consolidation and decommissioned the plant on the property, and the property sat vacant for a few years. It eventually became home to an asphalt and concrete recycling company that was not able to pay its taxes.

When CJ compared the property to other comps, it had an estimated value of $150,000 as raw land. The property had all of the building improvements removed from it. The biggest problem with the property was that it had a bunch of abandoned raw material (asphalt and concrete chunks) on the property that would cost about $100,000 to haul away.

CJ won the auction for $44,000 and then had to find a way to come up with the funding to close the deal.

Someone CJ had met in one of the local real estate meetups he attended reached out to him with questions about self-storage and to ask CJ's thoughts on a facility he was looking to buy. They ran through the numbers and had a great conversation about the investment. At the conclusion of that conversation, he thanked CJ for his time and asked him if there was anything he could do for him.

CJ mentioned the property that he had just won at auction. Being a fairly low dollar amount compared to most real estate, the risk to the lender was pretty low, and it turns out CJ's friend had enough funding available in his self-directed IRA. He agreed to fund a little more than the purchase price, allowing CJ enough cash to cover all costs associated with the transaction.

Crunch the Numbers:

Purchase price:	$45,000
After repair value:	$150,000 (just land with no improvements)
Term:	12 months guaranteed interest even with early refinance
Rate:	0 percent interest
Payment:	Interest-only payment, with balloon at 12 months

The challenges came even before CJ closed on the property. There were tons of raw materials on the property he needed to dispose of to make the property have any real value. If he could find a way to get the raw material removed at a reasonable price, the property would easily have over $100,000 in equity, in addition to the possibility of adding buildings and increasing the valuation even further.

Now, it's time to get excited. Look at how CJ creatively crushed this investment. Once he won the auction, CJ contacted the guy responsible for operations at the asphalt and concrete recycling company. CJ agreed to let them process the remaining material and sell it over the next four months without paying rent. The company also agreed to be responsible for any costs associated with the removal of the material and to pay a monthly lease for the space at the end of the term if any material remained.

The prior owner-operator got all of the raw material processed and cleaned up and decided to rent a single sliver of the property for the next year while the remainder of the material was sold and a place to move their equipment was found. Their lease amount covered all of CJ's holding costs, and the removal of the raw material resulted in a gain in equity of over $100,000 in less than six months

The private lender had very little risk in the deal. CJ personally guaranteed the loan for the lender to further remove risk. He had plenty of cash reserves in his accounts, which helped him qualify for bank loans and refinances. Using a private moneylender allowed CJ to keep his funds where the bank could see them while significantly growing his balance sheet.

Further, with the vast majority of the land cleared and unrented, CJ was able to develop a business-to-business relationship with a local boat rental company. As this boat rental company pulled boats out of a nearby lake, they winterized them and offered storage. CJ charged them a flat rate for each boat they stored over the winter, allowing them to mark it up and have another revenue stream during the winter, which is their slow time. CJ only had to manage one person coming in and out of the property. CJ plans to assist the boat rental company on marketing their storage offering in the years to come, and he projects that he will make $15,000 to $20,000 per year off of the property.

He now has the ability to go to a bank and get a construction loan that will leverage the equity in the property, which will allow him to build covered storage and potentially offer other storage which could exponentially increase the annual revenue off of the property, all without tying up any of his funds.

This was made possible by finding multiple win-win situations. His private lender was able to safely and securely invest funds. CJ was able to keep his cash reserves in place and gain equity which will allow him to easily refinance out of the private loan when he is ready. The prior operator of the business was able to process and sell the material, and CJ didn't have to pay to have it removed. A local boat rental company found a new revenue stream that helps them cover their costs in the off season.

Crunch the Numbers:

Purchase price:	$44,000
Repair costs:	$0
All-in number:	$45,000, after title costs and lender policy
Interest rate:	10 percent
Private lender profit:	$4,500
Borrower equity gain:	$105,000
Borrower cash gain:	$250 per month for year one; $1,200–$1,600 per month for year two
Rate of return to lender:	10 percent or better if CJ refinances early to roll into another deal
Rate of return to investor:	Infinite

4. Being a private moneylender will give you returns that are typically more stable than the stock market.

Everybody knows how blue chip stocks have performed. Who wouldn't like to have gotten in on a company like Apple, Amazon, or IBM on the ground floor? If you could go back in time with your checkbook to the days of those IPOs, how many shares would you buy?

The stock market can be a reliable long-term investment strategy, but it has its drawbacks. The first is that most stocks aren't Apple, Amazon, or IBM. Those are the exceptions. Most stocks, even the ones that generate wealth over years and decades, will never sniff the rare air that those stocks breathe.

Plus, in order to make real money in the stock market, you have to get in early, like as soon as the bell rings on the day they go public. If you wait too long, you will be chasing the people who got in early, the ones who will make the real money.

Even the best stocks can have a rough road. This is especially true with certain categories of stocks, like technology and automobile manufacturing. Amazon plodded along for years before it started to turn a profit. Anyone who has followed GM's stock prices over the years knows what a roller coaster ride that has been.

For all the love that cryptocurrency has gotten, all it took was for one country to decide it didn't like it and the price of one crypto dropped by four percent.

Uncertainty in the stock market or with cryptocurrency isn't always a bad thing. It's part of what helps people make a lot of money trading stocks. They buy low, sell high, and pocket the difference. The sooner and more extreme those differences occur, the more money people make and the quicker they get it.

The problem is that swings in the stock market can happen quicker than you think. Sometimes, all it takes is a few hours for the market to turn around. If you take a break for lunch or go to a movie, things can be different by the time you're done. That can mean you missed out on opportunities to buy a sweet deal or that you missed the right time to dump something.

The only way to avoid this pressure of the ups and downs of the stock market, or to be sure that you make as much money as you can, is to watch it like a hawk, seven days a week. You can't afford to look away if you want to make real money.

It gets crazier. You don't have to worry only about the stock markets in New York. This is a global game, and what happens overseas can take money out of your pocket.

Suppose a major real estate company in Asia fails to make a payment on a loan to a major bank or just looks like it's in a financial position where it can't make the payment. You might think, *Who cares? That's a billion miles away and doesn't matter to me.* If you have money in stocks, that would be the wrong attitude to have. All the stock markets are tied together, and what happens with one will impact the others. Therefore, if the real estate company in Asia doesn't make its payment, guess what's going to happen when the NYSE opens up the next morning? You got it. There's going to be a correction, which is a polite way of saying that people who aren't paying attention are about to lose a ton of cash.

The only way to avoid this is to be one of the big boys, one of the heavy hitters that can make some changes on their end to cover any potential losses. However, most of us will never be in that position. We will never have the kind of financial clout it takes to cushion our losses like that.

The only way most investors will be able to keep from getting swept up in the financial storms that start overseas is to watch the markets every minute of every day of the week. If you want to invest in the stock market, kiss your wife and kids goodbye.

Another benefit of being in real estate, especially as a private moneylender, is that you give up that instability. You don't have to sleep with one eye open wondering if something that is happening overseas will take money out of your pocket.

There is some risk with investing in real estate, and there is some volatility, but it's nothing like what happens with the stock market. Even during the global COVID pandemic, real estate remained a safe and steady way to invest. Despite the financial crisis that impacted many people, most tenants were able to pay their rent on time. In fact, most of the issues that impact real estate values are seen long before they show up and put real estate investments at risk. You can see a real estate bust coming in advance, and you have the chance to make changes to your portfolio if you need or want to.

CASE STUDY
Brighton Godwin

Brighton started his real estate career at the age of twenty in Edmond, Oklahoma, and built a portfolio of rental property worth over $1,000,000 by the time he was twenty-five. Brighton didn't go to college to learn how to run a company. He started building businesses in his senior year of high school by researching online and networking as much as he could. Brighton has worked in many industries and professions to learn what it takes to become a successful entrepreneur, including working in luxury car detailing, in contracting, and becoming a cable technician.

If you think a lack of cash keeps you out of the real estate game, read the next case study. On one deal, Brighton borrowed 100 percent of the purchase price, $75,000, from a private lender. He only had to bring $92 to closing. That is not a typo. This real estate stud bought a property and paid less than some people drop at Starbucks in a month.

The property was already rented for $700 a month, but Brighton knew it was worth more than that. Over a two-month period, he increased the rent to $900 a month. That was the biggest challenge he faced on the deal, and he resolved it by working with the tenant to increase the rate over a period of time instead of all at once. Plus, the tenant had been there for ten years and had five dogs, and Brighton wanted to find a way to keep him.

Within three months of buying the property, he refinanced the property with a national lender. Brighton knew what he was doing because the property appraised at $120,000 instead of his estimated $100,000, as-is value. The terms were for twelve months at eleven percent interest with six points. If he paid back the loan within six months, he paid four points. Brighton received $4,500 in cash at closing after paying the property taxes and $4,000 to another private lender. His monthly profit is about $250 after mortgage, taxes, insurance, and maintenance. Cha-ching!

He paid back his private lender within three months of borrowing the funds, which gave the private lender confidence in Brighton's business strategy and made them want to lend him more money on future deals.

Crunch the Numbers:

Purchase price:	$75,000
Repair costs:	$0
Interest rate:	11 percent
Private lender profit:	$5,250
Brighton's profit:	$4,400 from the refinance, plus $250 per month income
Rate of return to lender:	7 percent
Rate of return to investor:	Infinite

5. Being a private moneylender means you have the freedom to invest at your own pace or comfort level.

Now that I've caused half of you to start wondering why you ever opened an E*TRADE or Robinhood account, let's look at what this means to you as a private moneylender. Investing your money in someone else's real estate projects allows you to control how much you invest at a time and only in projects that make you feel comfortable. You get to control how much you spend, when you spend it, and what you spend it on, and you don't have a lot of pressure from outside influences.

Most other investment opportunities don't give you choices like that. If you put your money into a mutual fund, you have no control over how it is spent. You have to rely on the manager of the fund to put the money where it should be, which is where it will help you make the most money. If you think they are making a mistake and putting your money at risk, guess what your options are: none. You could only pull your money out and invest it somewhere else, but who wants to spend all that time and energy looking for another place to put money? If you put it in another mutual fund, you might be right back where you started.

Other opportunities have a high barrier to entry and might require you to invest a certain amount to get into the game. Want to buy a share of Bitcoin? Feel free to hand over more than $30,000 dollars (at least currently). That's great if you have the cash to do that deal and the confidence that Bitcoin is legit and will keep making money in the future. However, a lot of people don't know if cryptocurrency is a real deal or if it's just going to be a memory in a few years.

Being a private lender gives you the freedom to control when and how you invest. Here's the short version of how it works. Once investors know you are lending money to finance their goals of buying properties, people will come to you with proposals. They will want to borrow money to build their portfolios, and they will ask you for different amounts. Some may want to buy a single-family residential property, and others may need to finance the purchase of a large apartment complex. The point is you will have choices. If you want to start small, you can do that. If you want to jump into the deep end, try to build your empire as quickly as possible, and throw everything into one apartment complex, you can. Good for you! I admire your hustle. Rock stars like you make the world go 'round.

It's liberating to have that kind of freedom. You get to take control of your future, and you don't have to play by anybody else's rules. You can invest as much or as little as you want, and you don't have to answer to anybody about it. If the time is right for you, you can jump in with both feet, but if it doesn't feel like the right time, you can sit it out until the right deal comes along.

Plus, you will get to meet the people who want to do business with you. If they feel like a good fit, great. Make it happen. If not, pass on them until you meet an investor who checks off all of your boxes. It's as easy and straightforward as that.

CASE STUDY
Matt Blagg

Matt Blagg is a husband, father, singer/songwriter, worship leader, coach, and real estate investor. He lives in Edmond, Oklahoma, and spends time with his family whenever possible. He loves to be outside in God's creation, hiking, backpacking, and biking. He is a pilot and enjoys flying and anything related to aviation. That has come in handy with several real estate deals. He enjoys learning, considers himself a work in progress, and tries to improve in all areas of his life. He values teamwork, collaboration, and bringing others along with him.

In 2000, his father-in-law gave him a copy of *Rich Dad Poor Dad*, and he realized he needed to learn more about money and assets if he ever wanted to retire and be financially free.

In 2007, at the age of forty and after being on the road for eighteen years as a singer/songwriter, he flipped his first house. Despite making mistakes, he still made a decent profit. Since then, he has done several flips and even moved a house from Edmond to Norman, which is about sixty miles (he probably won't do that again).

He bought his first buy-and-hold in 2016. He wishes he would've started sooner with buy-and-hold, but he feared the unknown. Wholesaling has been a part of his strategy over the last couple years.

He has made mistakes (none fatal) and has learned from every deal he has done. His wife stopped teaching school and is joining him in the real estate business, which has been a long-term goal of his. "We are able to accomplish more together," he says.

An attorney friend of his, with whom he has had many conversations, mentioned that he was interested in real estate but has no experience. Matt offered to give him eight percent simple interest, secured by the property, which they were all in at seventy percent (simple interest means the borrower only pays interest on the principle, not any accumulated interest). Most loans are financed with compound interest, which is the Eighth Wonder of the World. Matt planned on doing a flip on a single-family brick house built in the early 1990s that needed a cosmetic makeover.

The offer was better than what his money was making and was a step for him to get into real estate. Matt also agreed to pay a full six-month term, even if he paid it off quicker, which keeps private lenders wanting to do repeat business. Matt made one lump sum payment at the end of the term, rather than making interest payments along the way. He has done this both ways but prefers to make one payment at the end.

Matt ran into a challenge on this property with an unexpected slab leak that required more cash. Thankfully, the lender had funds available outside a self-directed IRA. Matt called his go to plumbing and leak detection guy and got two other quotes. Matt presented them to the lender and got an extra $5,000 on the same terms.

The results were win-win, and this private lender offered to do more business together with Matt.

Crunch the Numbers:

Purchase price:	$115,000
Repair costs:	$35,000
All-in number:	$150,000
Interest rate:	8 percent
Private lender profit:	$6,000
Matt's profit:	$31,000
Rate of return to lender:	8 percent
Rate of return to investor:	Infinite
ARV:	$245,000
Potential rental income:	$2,000 or more

6. If done right, lending money from your IRA can be tax-free.

Being a private moneylender gives you a lot of flexibility, and it gives you options other investment opportunities can't. But wait. There's more. The best part is if you do it right, you can take money out of your IRA, tax-free, and use that to be a private moneylender. The short version is that by converting your IRA, Roth IRA, or 401k to a self-directed IRA, you can take that money and lend it to investors and make a greater profit than you would have made by leaving it where it is. You can do that tax-free. You won't have to pay any penalties when you take out the money, and it's tax-free when the loan is repaid with profits from your loans. However, be sure the loans are in compliance with statutes, or Uncle Sam will come looking for his slice of the pie, and that could include losing your entire IRA.

If you are lucky enough to be in a situation where your employer has matched your IRA contributions, you have hit a home run. You are going to be able to use that free money to bankroll deals with investors and make a pile of cash. Is there anything better than being able to use free money to make even more money? If you know of anything, let me know, but I don't expect to hear from any of you.

7. Being a private moneylender gives you control over how your money is spent.

Let's go one further. You can tell I like being a private moneylender and using private money to make things happen.

What is the real estate game all about? Execution.

If you want to talk about how great things are going to be some day, that's fine, but don't waste my time by talking and not taking any action. Private money lending is a way that doers, not talkers, build empires and give themselves and their families the lives they deserve.

I would say being a private moneylender gives you as much control as any other form of investing. You decide who you work with, when you work with them, and how much of your money you trust them with. You don't have to rely on a committee at a bank to decide if you get to make money or not, and if you think the real estate market is heading south, you can pull the plug on lending. It's all up to you. You get to make all the decisions, and you get to reap all the benefits.

What gives you more control than that? Sure, you have some control if you invest, especially if you are a day trader. You can pull your money out if you want, but there may be penalties involved, and you have to spend every waking moment determining when to buy and when to sell. If you use a broker to handle your investments, you have to wait for him to get your message, do a little a bit of research to figure out what you are talking about, and trade or sell your stocks.

That's not the end of the types of screw-ups that can happen when you invest in the market. Your broker may spend time telling you that selling is a bad idea, and you should wait it out because the market will turn soon, and you will get your money back at some point in the future. Plus, he may try to steer you into buying another stock, one you might not have even heard of—all while you are watching the stock price drop like a pound of lead into the deep end of a pool. You have to act quickly to keep your money from drowning, but the guy on the other end of the phone only seems to be worried about keeping your money in his account so that he can take his wife to the Caribbean again.

Where else can you put your money? Gold? Cryptocurrency? In a mason jar under your Aunt Mable's front porch? Those options may sound tempting, but they may not give you the ability to make a ton of cash on your terms. Aunt Mable's porch may be a safe place, but you won't make any money by depositing with her. Stocks, gold, and Bitcoin are long-term strategies. You may see a decent return in years or decades, but you probably won't make a lot of money in weeks or months, and you will have to rely on a lot of other people and circumstances beyond your control.

If you're looking for a way you can control who you work with, when you invest, and what types of investments you are involved in, and you want to invest in the hopes of making as much money as possible, you need to be a private moneylender.

CASE STUDY
Al Williamson

Al Williamson is a civil engineer who has been a traditional landlord in Sacramento since 1996. He started by buying a triplex, living in the smallest unit, and renting out the other two apartments.

In the following years, he created a corporate housing company that offered furnished rentals to business travelers who came to Sacramento for several months at a time. The company purchased a retail and mixed-use building, and they needed to fix it up to operate out of it.

Because the building was nearly completely vacant, they weren't able to get a traditional loan, so he turned to private money to get $400,000 to rehab the building.

He found loans through several private investors using their retirement accounts. His terms were ten percent interest only insured for twelve months with extensions. The challenges he faced were keeping the lenders up to date on progress and providing extensions to retirement account custodians. In order to handle this, he created monthly progress videos and emailed them to all the investors. This kept them informed and engaged.

He found that private money to be a way to build relationships with a group of small investors, so they could do bigger deals in the future. Over the years, he has learned that when there is an economic downturn and real estate prices drop, banks don't want to make loans. He is ready for the next downturn and is now in a position to go on a buying spree knowing he has cash from an army of private lenders.

They were able to rehab the building without using too much of their own money. They will refinance the entire building after it's fully occupied and performing. This way, they will be able to pay off the original loan holders, return the private capital they borrowed, and be ready for the next deal that comes along.

Crunch the Numbers:

Terms:	$100,000 down payment, and seller finances the balance at 4.3 percent
Purchase price:	$775,000
Repair costs:	$400,000
All-in number:	$1,175,000
Interest rate:	10 percent, interest only on repair cost private unsecured
Private lender profit:	22 private lenders of various amounts that range from $1,000 to $50,000 (unsecured) and a $100,000 secured loan on a different piece of property
Return to investor:	10 percent, mostly unsecured interest only

8. As a private moneylender, you get to control who you invest with.

You might be thinking that you *always* have control over who you invest with. After all, you don't send someone a check without knowing who they are and what they do. However, even if you know someone in the process, like a broker, you don't know everyone who will become responsible for your money. Your local broker is probably only the face for a big company, and he has to report to his boss, and that guy has to report to his boss, and so on and so on, until they eventually report to a board of directors or shareholders. So, where do you fit into all of that? How much power does your local broker actually have? Wouldn't it be nice if you were able to sit down face-to-face, eye-to-eye, with all of the people who will make decisions about how your money will be invested? If you have questions or want more information, wouldn't it be great to be able to make one phone call to the person you invested with?

There is a lot of peace and comfort in knowing who you are working with. I sleep better knowing that if I want to know about a house that my money was used to buy, I can just get in my car, drive across town, and make sure my money is still working for me.

That's another beautiful thing about being a private moneylender. Before you agree to do any deal, you meet the people who want to do business with you. You get to look them in the eyes, get a sense of who and what they are, and decide if they are the kinds of people you want to do business with. If you like them, great. You can sign the check and the agreement and let the investor help you build your empire. You can go home, or on vacation, and let the money flow in.

If they are not the kinds of people you want to do business with, you can walk away and let them find someone else. Either way, you can sleep well knowing that your money is safe. You have that confidence because you are the one who qualified the people you do business with, and you know how to track them down if you need to.

CASE STUDY
Patrick Grayson

Patrick Grayson has been in the real estate game his entire life. He is a third generation real estate investor and contractor from Carmel, Indiana, who has seen a lot of good, bad, and ugly investments. He started helping his dad paint rental properties when he was about seven and was paid in ice cream cones.

After growing up working on his parents' rentals, he spent ten years working for a Fortune 100 general contractor, then jumped into flipping houses and buying rentals. Patrick did live-in flips while he had a full-time job, and in 2017, Patrick became a full-time investor.

After working with contractors who cut corners, ran off with money, and lied, he had seen enough. He started Stolco Designs, a full-service, investor-friendly general contracting company serving the greater Indianapolis area. Patrick now manages his own rental portfolio and runs the office for a remodeling company that rehabs about fifty houses a year.

One flip stands out. Big jobs have never scared Patrick, and he liked the fact that there was less competition with the bigger jobs. They tore the roof off and built a second story to the house, converting it from a two-bedroom, one-bathroom home to a four-bedroom, two-bathroom home, as well as doubled the square footage. It was a project full of lessons learned, including permitting, private money, and lawsuits.

The private lender was a business acquaintance he had gotten to know over the few years their companies had worked together. He called Patrick one day and asked, "Hey, are you still doing that real estate stuff?"

"Yup. You wanna make some money together?" he asked. The rest is history. They now partner on a few deals each year.

Patrick likes to keep things simple. They wrote a one-page contract defining the role of each partner and outlining the investment terms. His friend lent the majority of the funds, and in return, he got a one percent origination fee and twenty percent of the net profit of the deal. There were no payments, just a profit share payable when the deal closed.

Right out of the gate, they shifted gears and decided to pop the top instead of doing a simple remodel. That meant the budget shot up (which is why Patrick kicked money into the deal), and the schedule stretched out. They decided it was worth it, but Patrick earned his stripes on this flip. The short story is they hired a general contractor who ended up being a textbook crook. They spent the next eighteen months, and about $30,000, in court. They won, though it didn't feel like it.

After that fiasco, Patrick just kept going. When the contractor was kicked off the job, he threw on his tool belt and hired a helper. They finished the house and got it listed. After that, he sought advice and guidance from more experienced investors and got a good lawyer.

This was a textbook simple private money deal. It also proves that private money contracts don't need to have complicated terms. At the end of it, the lender was thrilled and hounded Patrick to find another deal. Patrick loved it because it was one of his first private money deals, and it opened his eyes to the potential. Here is what you can do with private money, in real world terms. After this deal, the lender upgraded his Corvette. Patrick took the money and snagged a rental house. To this day, they still do deals together, and Patrick considers it a success that everyone made a chunk of change on the deal.

Crunch the Numbers:

Purchase price:	$60,000
Repair costs:	$86,000
All-in number:	$146,000
Interest rate:	20 percent of net profit, plus 1 percent origination fee
Private lender profit:	$12,000
Patrick's profit:	$44,000
Rate of return to lender:	14 percent over nine months

9. Private lending gives you a relatively quick turnaround on your investment.

If you are reading this book, you know that the name of the game in real estate is to make money. You want to find ways to make your bank account grow as quickly as you can. If you are really into the game, you eliminate everything you can that isn't helping you grow your empire. While other people waste time and energy watching television shows, you're looking for deals and try to find revenue streams to add to your portfolio. You're doing all the things other people aren't willing to do. That is the only way to build an empire.

Before you break out your checkbook, you need to know how much money you stand to make and how quickly you can get it—the quicker the better. This is another reason to become a private moneylender. You can make a great return on your investment much faster than you can with almost any other kind of investment.

This is especially true if you lend money to investors who are flipping houses. Most deals are done within six to twelve months, which means you get in and get out with a nice profit to show for it.

Flippers are my kind of people. They understand how to make money from real estate. They look for houses that need work, put some sweat equity into them, and sell them as quickly as they can. They aren't looking to hold onto properties for years and collect rent each and every month. They aren't interested in holding onto properties for decades to profit off the appreciation. To most flippers, speed is the name of the game. They want to maximize profits and minimize time. Their priority is to turn properties as soon as possible, and that means opportunities are open to you.

If investors go to a traditional brick-and-mortar bank to borrow money, you now know the hurdles they will have to go through. There are forms to fill out, documents to provide, and maybe even inspections that have to be performed. Investors, especially flippers, don't have the luxury of waiting for a committee to decide if they deserve to get a loan. They need cash, and they need it now. If they don't, they may not get the property they want, and that means they will lose money. Nobody wants that.

Investors operate quickly when they get money. They buy a property, flip it, pay off their lenders, and move on to the next deal. They don't waste a lot of time, and they won't put up with bank policies and procedures that slow them down.

All of this is a long way to say that if you are a private moneylender, you will be working with people whose goals are to turn over properties as quickly as they can. They won't get paid until you get paid, and that means you are probably looking at getting a sweet ROI in weeks or months, instead of years. It's a sweet deal, unless you're not interested in making a lot of money as fast as you can.

CASE STUDY
Jared Benjamin

Jared Benjamin is from Monroe, Louisiana, and has been in the real estate game for thirteen years. He's also a full-time deputy sheriff. Jared has a passion for all aspects of real estate. He became a licensed Realtor at the age of twenty and kept his license until he started on the buy-and-hold side in 2017. He began flipping and is in the process of build-to-sale. This journey has allowed him to see the power in real estate and how it can benefit everyone.

Jared was seeking money to buy a used car lot. He reached out to a doctor who is a family friend and presented him with an overview of the business and how the funds would be allocated.

They agreed on a $20,000 investment with a ten percent return. Monthly payments would be deferred for one balloon payment on or before the twelfth month, and there was no early payment penalty.

Their biggest challenge was determining how to move the money. Would the money come from an IRA or be cash or check? The lender decided to use cash because it was the easiest for him at the time.

Going to a bank was not an option as banks were not interested in giving lines of credit to small dealerships. Private money was an option that benefited both parties and had less red tape to combat.

Crunch the Numbers:

Purchase price:	$20,000
Interest rate:	10 percent
Private lender profit:	$2,000

That deal was the start of a good business relationship with the lender, and it provided Jared with an opportunity to work with his son as a private moneylender on a land flip.

Another deal called for ten percent down, and the private lender needed to put some money down. The purchase price of the land was $85,000. Jared needed a loan for the down payment. His private moneylender wanted to lend him the money with no questions asked. Jared agreed to pay him back $9,350 at the close of the sale or in six months, whichever came first.

Because they had worked together in the past, they both knew what needed to be done. The lender brought Jared a cashier's check for the down payment. They closed on the property the same day. In a matter of hours, the private lender made $850 on a one-percent origination fee.

Jared put the land on the market, and within five months, he sold it for $112,000.

Having a deal that went this smoothly gave him the opportunity to build trust and a stronger relationship with that private moneylender.

Following the success of those deals, they have now become partners in a laundromat and in billboard businesses.

10. When you are a private lender to real estate investors, your loans are secured.

This just keeps getting better. Private lending is a great way to make money in a controlled way with people you trust, but you really don't need a whole lot of trust. I can hear some of you yelling as you read that, but trust can be built in a lot of ways. You can trust people by knowing that their word means something and that they do what they say they are going to do. You solve that problem by meeting with people and doing business only with people you have vetted.

Another way to build trust is to make the deals bulletproof by ensuring you will be paid, regardless of what happens.

How do you do that?

You let the investor do all the work. When word gets out that you are a private moneylender, investors will start calling you to set up deals. Some of them will be wannabes or rookies trying to get that first deal done. There's nothing wrong with that, and if they make you a sweet deal that helps you build your empire, jump on it like a duck on a June bug. However, the pros, the ones who have been at this a while, will bring you opportunities that you can't, and shouldn't, resist.

The only deals you should do look something like this: An investor has found a smoking deal on a property, one that stands to make you both a lot of money. It needs work, or a family is trying to dump it because it belonged to Uncle Frank who just passed away. No one wants to put in the time or money to fix it up. The investor has crunched the numbers, and he needs to borrow less money than the house is worth. He comes to you, gives you the before comps and all the paperwork, and you look it over. The comps, or comparables, are the values of similar properties in the same area.

If you lend him what he is asking, he needs to give you a lien on the property, one that is worth less than the value of the loan. Even if things go south and the deal winds up in the toilet, you will get your money back by selling the house. Therefore, there's no way to lose money on the deal, assuming you do your homework, and the right paperwork gets filed. The only things to think about are how much money will you make and how quickly will you make it.

What happens if the stock market goes south? Will you own any assets that can be sold to give you your investment back? If all that cryptocurrency you've bought takes a nosedive, and your money is gone, who is going to care? You will be on your own with no secured property to protect yourself.

Being a private moneylender is one of the best ways to invest because it is one of the few ways to have an investment secured by real property, something you can see and touch, something that can be sold if it needs to be. Even banks respect this concept. Imagine if you walked into a bank and asked for money to buy stocks. Their laughter would still be ringing in your ears when you get home. However, if you show them a deal that is secured by real property, they will roll out the red carpet.

It is important to get your paperwork in order. Every deal is secured by a mortgage or deed of trust, and if things go south, the property can be sold. A mortgage is a loan that is secured by a piece of real estate, while a deed of trust happens when property is transferred to a trustee who holds it as security for a loan between a buyer and a seller. One good thing about using a deed of trust is that it can be split among several investors, which is another great way to protect your investment and minimize your risk.

Even though lenders secure deals with property, they have to be the right deals with the right investors. The loan-to-value ratio should never be more than seventy to eighty percent, and the loan-to-cost ratio (LTC) shouldn't be more than eighty percent. For example, if a property is valued at $100,000, the loan-to-value should never exceed $70,000. Loan-to-cost is the number of debt dollars divided by the total cost of a project. If the ratio is higher than eighty percent, it's a sign the property is over leveraged.

Private lenders who secure their loans with real property can also be called hard moneylenders, but that term usually applies to people who are full-time moneylenders.

Another great aspect of private lending is that your money is backed by collateral. It's not some random number or tiny percentage of an intangible investment. When you lend private money, you can visit the building that secures it. If you want, you can even get out of your car and touch it, but I wouldn't recommend that, especially if it's in a bad neighborhood or late at night. Those things tend to freak people out.

CASE STUDY
Liz Poteet

Liz lives in Oklahoma and describes herself as "a non-risk-taking woman in her late fifties." She has four grown children who all went to college and took her money with them. After hustling for college tuition, books, and fees for four kids over fifteen years, she finally settled down to breathe. Realizing that she was close to retirement, she started looking at the funds she had set aside for herself. There was not nearly enough to support her for any length of time. Retirement age is sixty-seven, and if she lived much longer than that, she would be living on her social security income. That would mean she would have to eat a lot of beans and rice. Nobody wants that.

For eight years, she has been working with a real estate investor who seems to have a knack for making money. Liz was looking for a way to increase her retirement savings without taking a major risk, and her boss suggested she try private money lending. He even set her up with her first deal.

A couple approached her boss stating their home was in foreclosure. They needed money to pay off the mortgage and make improvements required to refinance. They were determined to get themselves back on a solid financial track. Liz's boss offered her the deal, and she reluctantly accepted.

First set of numbers:

Private money loan amount:	$100,000
Home value:	$151,000
Origination fee:	$2,500
Document fee:	$45
Interest rate:	12 percent
Term:	12 months

The first challenge Liz faced was convincing herself to actually let go of the money. The second challenge she faced was learning what documents she needed to make the deal happen and to keep her investment secure.

Convincing herself to let go of the money was easy. She had the opportunity to lend money with no risk. The house appraised for significantly more than the loan. If the borrowers could not repay the loan, she could sell the house and still make a profit. Knowing that made it easier for her to sign the check.

Making sure she had all the correct documents was also pretty straightforward. She worked daily with a successful real estate investor, and he was willing to help her achieve her goals. If she didn't have his help, she would have hired a real estate attorney to protect her investment.

The deal was interesting to Liz because she had the opportunity to make a private money loan with no risk involved. The other thing that made this deal appealing was the ability to help a couple save their family home.

Liz ended up spending about five hours of her time preparing the loan documents, filing the proper paperwork, and closing the deal. With her time included, it cost her $545 to make this deal happen.

Crunch the Numbers:

As you can see by the numbers below, the private money loan was highly profitable with very little work.

Income:	$12,000 in interest; $2,500 origination fee
Total income:	$14,545
Expenses:	Time expenses: $500; document fees: $45
Total expenses:	$545
Net profit:	$14,000
ROI:	14.55 percent

The family was able to get their home out of foreclosure, do the needed repairs, and refinance their home with a traditional bank at a better interest rate. They also created a new financial plan for the future.

11. In real estate investing, there is an immediacy that benefits everybody.

We've already talked about this, but with seasoned investors, there is pressure to get deals done as quickly as possible. They can't afford to wait for money to start flowing to them. If they go to a bank or talk to a private moneylender, they have a deal in the works. That means they need money yesterday. You will never hear a serious investor tell a lender, "I've been thinking I might buy a property in six months. I haven't found anything yet, but I think I will start looking in the spring. I'm here to get preapproved so that I will have the money when I need it. Break me off a piece, so I can put it in my back pocket and have it ready when I decide I want to make more money."

If an investor said that, I think most bankers and private moneylenders would say something like, "Thanks for wasting my time. Come back when you can show me a viable deal, one that I can crunch the numbers on to see if we can both make money."

Lenders aren't interested in something that may happen at some unknown time in the future. They only want to invest in deals that are happening now.

The good news is that most serious investors have the same mindset. They want to make money today, and they don't want to waste their time or anyone else's if they don't have a deal they think will work.

If some investor does come to you with the idea of borrowing money for a future deal that he doesn't have a property for, do yourself a favor and make sure he knows he wasted your time. In my book, he owes you lunch at the very least. I would collect that as soon as you can. Collect now because you may never see him again.

CASE STUDY
Shawn McVicker

Shawn lives in Minnesota, but he invests in Oklahoma City. He became interested in real estate at the age of twenty-two. He began wholesaling and did that for about six years, collecting a rental property here and there. By 2019, he had about eighteen rental properties. He bumbled through some rehabs, making money only because he was buying houses at deep discounts. His focus has shifted from wholesaling to predominantly buy-and-hold investing with some flipping for cash, which he uses as fuel for the business.

The first transaction he did with his current wife was her first deal, and it was before they were married. The deal was a lead that came from their direct mail campaign. It involved a man whose home was going to be sold at the county tax sale. The man had grown up in a trailer park and inherited a pile of money, but now that cash was gone. He couldn't keep up the big house he had bought and wanted enough money to buy a trailer where he could be comfortable.

He made a deal with his private lender for two percent origination and twelve percent interest, payable when we closed the sale of the property.

The tax sale for the property was about a week away. The pressure was on. After purchase, renovations began. It was a nice home that had not been kept up. There were mice and rats throughout, including in the attic. There was a strange smell that was all but gone when it came time to list the property. One person was willing to overlook the smell for a $5,000 price reduction, which Shawn agreed to.

The title company whipped up the title work in record speed, and their private lender had no trouble providing funds in time for a four- or five-day turnaround from contract to close.

For Shawn, it was nice not to deal with all the rigmarole from a bank. Everyone made money, and a business relationship was formed.

Crunch the Numbers:

Purchase price:	$53,000
After-repair cost:	$88,000
Interest rate:	12 percent
Private lender profit:	$5,600
Shawn's profit:	$57,200
Rate of return to lender:	12 percent

CASE STUDY
Greg Meech and Me

I grew up poor, so poor that my family didn't exchange gifts on Christmas. We didn't have a lot of stuff, and like any other child, I wanted things. I especially liked remote control (RC) cars. They were always in the back of my mind. I thought, *Maybe someday I can get one.* Finally, after being a real estate investor for about fifteen years, I had some money and jumped into remote control cars as a hobby. It was something I had always wanted to do, and with the money I was making in real estate, I could afford to indulge myself.

I frequently went to a place called 405 Raceway to drive my RC cars. I made a commitment to carve time out of my busy schedule to have fun, and this was my outlet for that.

After a while, I saw it as a networking opportunity. I purchased extra RC cars and invited other real estate investors to join me. It was a great experience.

I also befriended the owner of the RC car track, Gary O'Brien. Gary has dedicated his life to his RC shop. Gary's "real" job was with the postal service. When he retired, Gary used his retirement to invest in his dream of building an RC car store with an extremely elaborate racetrack with jumps on a platform that were twenty feet off the ground.

Gary and I saw each other almost every Wednesday, and we enjoyed each other's company. Gary is an entrepreneur, my favorite kind of person, and he didn't shy away from doing the work needed to make his dream become a reality. I encouraged Gary to achieve his goals, and I helped with marketing and whatever else I could do.

One day, Gary told me that he had to move out of the location where he had built his business because the owners of the building had sold it.

I was crushed. I felt this was sad for Oklahoma City because there was nothing comparable to what Gary had built. I didn't want my friend to lose his lifelong dream any more than I wanted to lose my favorite hobby.

My mind started racing. *Where in the world is this guy gonna go?* I thought. I made a commitment to Gary to find a building that would work for his RC store and track, and I called two real estate agents. One of them worked his tail off and found an 8,000-square-foot retail space on Northwest 23rd Street in Oklahoma City.

When I walked into the building, I knew it would be the perfect location. I was elated. However, the job wasn't done, and the Realtor and I had to put in some extra hustle. Gary had to move as soon as possible. There was no time for all the normal delays that come with purchasing commercial property.

This was a great opportunity. I was looking for a commercial property and had a tenant willing to sign a five-year lease and move in. All I had to do was find a building.

The real estate agent mentioned a bank he had been working with for some time that could expedite the closing of the building. He indicated the bank may close the loan without having to wait for the appraisal. I reiterated that we had to close by September 30th because I had a pre-signed lease with a five-year term for $5,000 per month. The Realtor reassured me that he could make it happen.

I went to the bank the Realtor had suggested and filled out the application. I specified that I wanted a no-money-down deal, so I could use my cash reserves to update the building. The loan agent at the bank looked over my application and financials and was confident they could close by the deadline. The agent assured me he would order an expedited appraisal, and they would be good to go.

As you may have guessed, that is not what happened. The banker had a scheduled vacation, which, by itself, was not an issue. The issue was that he forgot to order the appraisal before he left town.

Welcome, ladies and gentlemen, to the world of real estate investing.

My mind went crazy. I realized that we were getting down to the wire, and I had Gary's business in my hands. Gary had inventory that needed a home, and the banker and his three-piece suit were on vacation.

I did what I could. I called the bank several times a day asking what was happening with the loan. I had to close on the property as soon as possible and needed an update.

The appraisal finally came in, five days before the closing date. The building appraised for $650,000, and I had the property under contract for $475,000. I had crunched the numbers correctly and knew it would be a no-money-down deal.

I relaxed for a moment. Gary had trusted me to come through and to protect his livelihood. I was relieved to know that Gary's trust in me would not be broken. My word is my bond, and I couldn't stand the thought of letting him down. Plus, I love RC cars and didn't want Gary's business to go under or be forced to search for another location.

The closing was set for a Friday. On the Monday before, the banker did the unthinkable. He called to tell me that I would need to put twenty percent down. I was pissed, to say the least.

I reminded the banker that I had made it clear from the beginning that I wanted a no-money-down deal, so my cash reserves could be used to improve the building. The banker started giving me the runaround, a not so uncommon activity for bankers to do. It was one of the most gut-wrenching moments of my real estate investment career.

The banker put me in a desperate position. I had to close on the building in five days. I could fork over twenty percent, close with the bank, and accept the indifference to my specific requests concerning the loan, or I could find another way to make this deal happen. I decided I wasn't going to lay down for this. I had a smoking deal and didn't want it to go down the toilet.

I decided to close the deal using private money. I love having options. I emailed a friend in Houston, Greg Meech, someone I had been developing a relationship with for about five years. I laid out the details of the deal. The property was listed for $550,000, I had it under contract for $475,000, and it appraised for $650,000. Most importantly, the deal had to close in five days. I humbly asked if my friend would be interested in lending. His simple reply was, "How much and how long?"

I received the wired funds in plenty of time to close the deal. The deal closed that Friday, and Gary moved in.

That day changed my life. It gets better, though.

Within sixty days of that private money loan, I refinanced the property at a different bank and got better terms. It turned into a true no-money-down deal.

I did a triple net lease with Gary. Because of the size of the building, Gary was able to move his track, in pieces, to the new building. In all the years I've owned this property, I haven't had to put much money into it, other than repairing the rear parking lot.

Everybody won on this deal. My private lender was ecstatic that he made $5,000. Gary's family is able to spend countless hours playing with their RC cars. Gary was able to continue his dream almost without a hitch. It also blesses my real estate company because it has been cash flowing from day one.

This case study is a perfect example of how, in real estate, everyone needs to have options. You never know when a deal is going to fall into your lap, and private money can be an ideal option. Borrowers can generally get the money quickly, which can be the difference between doing the deal of a lifetime or losing the deal of a lifetime.

It also shows that there are private lenders out there if you take the time to find them and build relationships. If you have money to lend, there are investors out there looking for you, and you can make a great rate of return on your money.

12. There is a large pool of potential clients for private moneylenders.

Another great benefit about being a private moneylender is that there seems to be a never-ending pool of potential clients. A lot of people have jumped into the real estate game, and for good reason. People finally figured out it's a great way to build financial security, and it works for a lot of people. People who have been successful in one career, such as doctors and lawyers, have discovered it's a great way to invest their money. People who don't have college degrees figured out they can create wealth and financial security for themselves and their families by owning rental properties or flipping houses. It's a great industry, and if you are willing to hustle and learn, you can be successful in it, maybe even more successful than you dreamed of. That's what happened to me.

Regardless of education or success, what's the one thing every investor needs? You know this.

Every investor needs *cash*. They need reliable access to money they can use to buy property. They need greenbacks, Benjamins, bucks, cabbage, cheddar, or whatever you call it. Money is what allows any investor to grow, and as we all know, if you're not growing, you're dying. Borrowed money is the lifeblood for any investor, and without it, they will sink into the middle of the ocean with no life raft.

This is true even for investors who have a lot of money. There are a lot of reasons why it makes sense to use borrowed money to finance deals, but that's a conversation for another day. Trust me when I tell you there are plenty of people who need to borrow money, even people who have the cash in the bank.

In the past, where did people go to borrow money? The bank, of course.

Okay, maybe a few people had a friend who knew somebody who knew somebody who could, for ridiculous interest rates, bring you a brown paper bag full of cash. However, that's no way to build an empire. Miss one payment and you might be walking with a limp for the rest of your life.

Banks have never let money flow like water. They have always had to be responsible with their funds, but it has recently gotten worse. It's mostly their fault. In the early 2000s, they lent money to a lot of people who had no business borrowing. Banks approved loans that never should have been given, and you know the rest of the story of the subprime crisis. It wasn't long before reality set in, and people started defaulting on their loans.

It wasn't just one or two people. This was happening across the country, in almost every city and every state. It got so bad that banks had to be bailed out of the mess they helped to create.

As a result, regulations increased, and banks had to become stricter about who they lent money to. They couldn't just rubber stamp applications, and they had to be more stringent about how they documented the income of people who filled out loan applications. This means fewer people are now able to qualify for traditional loans.

There have been a lot of other events that have restricted people's ability to borrow from banks. In the wake of the COVID pandemic, a lot of people were forced out of work and struggled to pay their bills. Some people couldn't pay their rent, and this meant landlords across the country had their finances impacted as well. Most were honest and hardworking people who just found themselves in a bad spot.

Despite the fact that they did the best they could, what was the end result? They found themselves with dings on their credit scores, and we all know how banks feel about that.

A lot of people will no longer have access to traditional banks, at least in the short term, and this provides an opportunity to you as a private moneylender. It's a great way to help people build their dreams and also make a decent profit.

Another benefit is that these people will be grateful. They couldn't have gotten their deals done without you or someone like you, which just goes to show that private lending is a win-win situation.

There are other reasons banks don't want to get into a lot of real estate deals. First, banks don't like fixer-uppers, and they don't want to deal with the work it takes to get them ready for sale. Let's suppose you brought me a deal on a property you found. It needs work, but after I did the math and accounted for the sweat and money needed to be put into it, it would inevitably make a ton of profit. I would sign off on that deal in a heartbeat. I can even see us at the title office at closing with smiles on our faces because of the cash we just put in our pockets. If you find deals like that, hit me up. I'd love to get as many of those going as I can.

However, consider if you took that same deal to a bank. They would probably send an inspector out to the property, and when he came back with his report, you would get a call telling you they won't approve the loan. Banks aren't interested in potential. They don't care what might happen after you fix up the house. They only care about the comps on the property in the here and now. They aren't going to put money into something if they can't look through their traditional lenses and see how it all can work out.

Second, most banks are not interested in short-term loans for small amounts. They don't want to front someone cash for a few months. They want to sell people loans that last for fifteen or, preferably, thirty years. That's how they make their money. They want people dialed in for a long time, making payments month after month. That's how the interest piles up and how bankers get paid. Investors are sprinters. Bankers run marathons.

CASE STUDY
Kurt and Elizabeth Phillips

Kurt and Elizabeth Phillips are a husband-and-wife team from Lancaster, Ohio. They invest in buy-and-hold single- and multi-family homes in central Ohio. In addition to building a real estate empire, they also work together to educate their six children.

Kurt resigned from UPS when he was thirty-nine. He had been a package delivery driver for twelve years. They realized they were no longer "bankable," and that was a problem because they were going into real estate full-time. They also knew that investing with only their own money was a long and improbable road to financial freedom. Out of necessity, they discovered the power of private money. To say this investment strategy was life changing is an understatement. They now finance all of their acquisitions with private money, rehabbing homes to achieve market rent and market value. Once that is done, they refinance with local banks.

They bought their first duplex in 2003, living on one side for almost nine years and renting the other. It was their first private money deal.

The duplex was part of a seller's portfolio that included another duplex and a quadplex for a total of eight doors. They had the ability to purchase the quadplex and wholesaled the other duplex. There was another duplex in the portfolio, but they needed financing to get that done. The problem was that they were denied by every bank Kurt contacted. One bank told them they could fund the deal, only to withdraw their funding right before closing. That put Kurt and Elizabeth in a terrible spot, and they had only two options, assign the contract or find some private money to fund the deal.

Crunch the Numbers:

Purchase price:	$68,000
ARV:	$110,000
Terms:	12 percent interest only for 12 months, 0 points

Their biggest challenge was overcoming their fear and insecurities. Getting denied by several banks was rough. They had worked with one of the banks on two previous deals while Kurt was employed at UPS. Two potential private lenders also said no. Kurt was shaking with nerves and anxiety before making calls to banks and lenders. Getting the money wasn't the final hurdle. They also had to find a title company that was familiar with private lending. Kurt made numerous phone calls to find one that was the right fit.

They were at a point in their business where they had to make this deal work. It is amazing what can be done when our backs are against a wall. Desperation is a great motivator. Kurt took action, made calls, and kept pushing through the rude and haughty comments. A private lender finally said yes, and the deal got done. During that time, they hired a real estate coach.

His expertise and extensive connections proved to be pivotal to their growth.

They left that process feeling as if they had discovered the formula for working with private lenders. When the deal closed and was refinanced, their confidence and knowledge exponentially increased.

They became students of the process and dove into all the material they could find on private money, including books, courses, conferences, and coaching. With this newfound confidence and knowledge, the sky was truly the limit for them. After the deal went down with private money, they realized they could live the life of their dreams and achieve financial freedom. They have funded every deal since then with private money or seller financing.

After eleven months, they connected with a local bank that was willing to refinance the loan into a twenty-five-year fixed rate at 5.25 percent. This enabled them to pay back their lender in full and hold onto an asset that cash flows $687 monthly for their family.

They learned that networking is everything. If you network with integrity, doors will open. Carry yourself with confidence, even if you don't feel like you have it. Show up every single day. Don't be intimidated by bankers, lawyers, or inherited residents with large dogs.

Kurt and Elizabeth also learned that private lenders are normal people with real goals and real needs. It is key that you listen to their situations to craft an agreement that will be mutually beneficial. Know that you are offering an opportunity that is beneficial to the private lender, and be sure they are the kinds of people with whom you can work.

They learned to follow the laws of private lending, which include the importance of having an attorney review documents for your specific county and state. Don't just use information you find on the internet. Pay for legal counsel to do things correctly. Some of the main things you need to cover with your legal team are the interest rates you are allowed to charge, the documents you need to file to protect your money, a process for how to collect if the deal tanks, and a plan on whether or not you need to set up a corporation or other legal structure to lend money.

Be willing to pay for coaching, especially when you can't afford it. Interview and vet every coach carefully. Be sure they have the results and integrity you are seeking.

Don't limit yourself by borrowing only from local lenders. You can go nationwide and borrow money from across state lines.

Finally, be an excellent student. Do the homework, and follow the wisdom of those who mentor you. It's never easy, but it's possible.

CASE STUDY
JJ Gritts

JJ Gritts is a real estate investor who primarily invests in buy-and-hold single family real estate in Oklahoma City. In addition to buy-and-hold investing, he fixes and flips to acquire larger chunks of capital that he uses to help grow his business.

He has been investing since 2013 when he started building speculative (spec) houses with a partner to generate additional income for his family. He had dreams of eventually leaving his day job. In 2016, due to some unfavorable job changes, he jumped into real estate investing full-time. He primarily uses local banks to fund his deals, but from time to time, he partners with private lenders for financing.

He believes private lending can be done with transactions that are easy for everyone involved, but that can vary, based on the specifics of each deal. He has done deals in a variety of ways, including quick-in and quick-out bridge financing (usually lasting a month or less) to longer term loans (debt partnerships that are for one year or longer).

In 2020, he was acquiring properties at a rapid pace and was running into lending limits with his traditional bank because banks were capped on the amount they could lend each individual, based on the bank's size. In order to continue acquiring deals, he had to search for additional sources of funding. He had a fire property (it literally had been on fire) under contract and reached out to a friend who had previously inquired about lending him money. With one simple phone call and a short conversation about the deal and the terms, JJ acquired funding for his deal. His friend lent him $66,000 for one year at eight percent simple interest on a house that would be worth $120,000 once it was renovated.

JJ was able to buy the property for $28,000 from a very happy seller and gave his friend and lender a mortgage, promissory note, and first lien position on the property (all of which was handled by his title company), and the best part is JJ currently makes $440 a month in income.

After buying the property, JJ completely remodeled the house, rented it, refinanced it onto permanent financing with one of the local banks he typically used. He then paid his lender back the original $66,000. Everyone won on this deal.

Private lending can seem scary or complicated at first, especially when you haven't done it before, but as you can see from this story, it's simple and easy to do when you work with the right people.

Crunch the Numbers:

Purchase price:	$28,000
Repair costs:	$70,000
Interest rate:	8 percent
Private lender profit:	$5,280
Rate of return to lender:	8 percent (on $66,000 origination amount)
Rate of return to investor:	Infinite (after permanent refinance)

THE HOW

Now that you know why you should be a private moneylender, let's look at the how. Here are the steps you need to take to create a super profitable stream of revenue by lending money to real estate investors.

1. Get some money.

If you are reading this, you probably already have some. If not, learn how to be ready to invest when you have enough cash to start being a private lender.

How much money do you need? Not as much as you might think. If you have $5,000 to $10,000, you might be able to get in the game if you pool your money with other investors and act as a group. This is a great way to get started because you don't have to do it alone. You can work with other people and learn from them. You don't have to cut your teeth all by yourself.

Working with others is also a way you can invest as much as your comfort level or budget allows. It's a good way to make sure private money lending is a good fit for your portfolio and goals.

You might even have money that would be perfect for private money lending and not even know it. Many people have a 401k or retirement funds. What a lot of people don't know is that funds from those can be converted into a self-directed IRA, and that money with no penalties can be used to invest in real estate with no penalties to the IRA. The profits can be tax-free. Plus, the level of return you will get from real estate will probably be much higher than what the IRA is paying. This is a great way to get started as a private moneylender without having to struggle to find money to invest. You may already have it, and you just need to learn to move it around.

2. Build a structure.

Don't put your empire at risk by being in business without having some kind of formal shell in place to protect you and what you have built. In the unlikely event something goes wrong (if you do your due diligence, it probably won't), you don't want to lose sleep over the possibility of having your assets taken from you. Considering the protection and peace of mind that a business structure gives you, it is worth the cost. Depending on where you live, it may only cost a few hundred dollars to have an LLC or corporation created for you, and that is some of the cheapest insurance you will ever buy. If you are using a self-directed IRA, you may not even need this because you are using retirement funds. If you want to take your investing to another level, you will definitely need a legal structure at some point.

Once you have money ready to go, you're closer to increasing your empire. However, you don't want to make a move without having a structure in place. You need to have the right kind of business entity to make big things happen.

You need to consult with your attorney and advisors, but to be successful as a private moneylender, you may need to operate as an LLC, a corporation, or some other kind of entity.

3. Find investors who need cash.

This is when the magic happens, when you get to send your cash out into the world. It's where your mama and papa dollars start making baby dollars that all live in your bank account.

It sounds easy, but doing your first deal will involve a lot of leg work. You have to get out and hustle by making calls, meeting people, and knocking on doors. There is no easy way to live the life you have dreamed of. You have to be proactive to make it happen.

So, how can you find investors who need to pay you to borrow your money?

A. Investor clubs are a great place to start.

People who join investor clubs are front-line soldiers, the ones who battle every day to build empires. They need your cash, and they know it. Without cash from a lender like you, their businesses will die. In the real estate business, you are either growing or dying, and investors need cash to grow. This puts private moneylenders in an awesome position. Because investors need cash, and they know they need it, they are willing to pay you a hefty fee to borrow it. To make it even easier, borrowers don't care where the money comes from. They just want the ability to make deals happen, and that means having cash.

To private moneylenders, visiting investor clubs is like shooting fish in a giant prequalified barrel. You know they want to take the bait, and all you have to do is dangle the hook in front of them and wait for them to bite.

CASE STUDY
Andy Grieb and Me

This case study is probably the most exciting one to share because it's unique, and it benefited both parties in a lot of ways. Let me give you some history on how this all came about.

You want to go to your local real estate group or association, also known as a REIA, and connect with people. At one of the meetings I went to, I connected with an investor named Andy Grieb. Andy is a world traveler and has lived in several places. He was in the military and is now an airline pilot instructor. He started doing real estate five years before we met, which happened by accident because he had to move. At the time, he didn't know what to do with his home. He couldn't sell it because the market was low, and he didn't want to take a bath and lose out on his investment. He was forced to rent it out.

Over the years, he transitioned to different areas of the country and became an accidental landlord again. He realized he could make money doing that and visited a real estate club meeting in Oklahoma City. I overheard him at a meeting talking about private money with some people and struck up a conversation with them. Over time, we built a relationship.

Andy and I connected. He's savvy and said he had tax-free money to lend out of his IRA. I said I would one day take him up on that. He was a lot more educated and rehearsed in private lending than I was at that time. I found out he was also looking to borrow money to finance deals.

What makes this story more powerful for me than anything else? I pushed myself to borrow the money. I got used to using banks, and I don't like going outside my comfort zone because it's a process. One day, a Realtor called me about a property in Oklahoma City.

The address was 19 Northeast 65th, and it was listed for about $90,000. I went and checked out the property. It is a three-bedroom, two-bath, three-car garage property in Oklahoma City. The owners had passed away, and it was willed to somebody who didn't want to maintain it, manage it, or even update it.

I had an idea of what the property was worth. I made an offer for $69,000, and I got it. I was excited about that. It was a sweet deal, and I knew I was going to make money.

That was one of the first times I took my business to the next level as a private lender and as a borrower. I had the money lined up. I called my bank and ordered an appraisal. I always have multiple sources of funding ready to go. Options are powerful.

I learned early on to change banks from time to time. People in banks change, so you never know if the people you deal with will be working there when you need money. I wanted to be ready and prepared, so I pulled the appraisal on the property. The appraisal came back at $125,000. I knew I wanted to improve the property and increase the money I had invested in it from $69,000 to about $80,000.

I knew I could a borrow a hundred percent financing from the bank because I had established a relationship and have a lot of credit with them. However, for fun, I wanted to stretch myself by reaching out to Andy to see how the private lending process works on the borrower's side.

I texted the private lender and said, "I have this property. I know it's worth at least $125,000. I'm requesting $80,000." By the next day, he replied back and said he had already pulled comps.

The comps he pulled were $85,000, and that wouldn't work out because seventy percent of $85,000 wouldn't close the transaction as a no-money-down deal. I like to do no-money-down deals because there is always a margin in case something goes wrong.

I emailed him the appraisal I had received for $125,000, and I said, "I don't really need your money. I can borrow $93,000 from the bank and put even more money in my pocket, but I was trying to be conservative. I wonder if you would just lend me $80,000 for twelve months."

You can always negotiate with private lenders. He agreed to lend me the $80,000. He agreed to a one percent origination fee, though he normally charges two or three percent. He also agreed we could renegotiate after twelve months.

I was excited. The money came in two parts. He and his wife, April, both paid $40,000 out of their IRAs. I closed the transaction with no money down, and everything was great.

A little over a year later, I had forgotten about the loan. It was on auto pay, and we were fourteen months into it. I needed to cash out, but he was happy I was paying longer than anticipated because all of the money he received went directly to his IRA as tax-free money.

Right before the two-year mark, I paid him back, and everything was great. However, during that process, about six months into it, he called me and wanted to borrow $25,000 to buy properties in Buffalo, New York. The entire thing seemed bizarre to me.

He lives in Oklahoma City but flies around the world. I was borrowing $80,000 out of his IRA. He was asking me for $25,000 out of my IRA to help buy a package of properties in Buffalo, New York, worth several hundred thousand dollars.

Now it's 2022, and his deal has increased thirty or forty percent. He's going to make a huge return, and he's benefited all the way around. He got acquisition money. He closed his Buffalo transaction with no money down by using a couple of private lenders. He made money lending me money, and I made money when I lent money to him.

It has been an awesome process and a great relationship.

B. Develop relationships with bankers.

Another great way to find potential investors to lend money to is to have a few bankers on speed dial.

Why?

Who do most investors turn to when they need cash? Their banks, of course. Just like the rest of us, when investors need a loan, they get on the phone and call the loan officer at their bank. That makes sense, right? After all, that's the place with the big vaults where they keep all the cash.

However, the problem is it's getting harder and harder for most people to get loans from banks. As we already discussed, after the subprime mortgage crash that happened from 2007–2010, regulations changed. Before that, a lot of banks were rubber stamping loan applications. If people came in with completed applications and a pulse, some banks seemed to give out as much money as the people wanted. They weren't verifying income or the borrowers' abilities to repay. The only thing those banks cared about was getting the loan approved and making a commission. It was easy money, at least in the short-term. The problem was no one was thinking about the long-term impact of issuing loans that were certain to be defaulted on, or, if they were, they didn't care. It didn't bother anyone that they had lent money to people who had no way to repay it.

It didn't take long for those bad loans to hit the fan. People from across the country started defaulting, and this screwed up the entire banking industry. The federal government stepped in to make sure the entire financial services industry didn't crash.

The US Government didn't want that to happen again, so it passed laws and regulations that made it harder for banks to approve loans. They now have to verify income, and this has made it harder for people to borrow money. You have to practically give blood and jump through hoops. You have to document every penny you make, and if you can't do that, or if the numbers don't add up, you can forget about buying that new property. This has screwed over a lot of self-employed people and cut them out of borrowing money from traditional banks.

The good news is this has created opportunities for private lenders. Investors have one less place to turn to when they need to borrow cash.

How can you turn this into money in your pocket? If you have a relationship with bankers, let them know you are a private lender. If they know of any investors who don't qualify for traditional loans, tell them to call you. If you know enough of the right people in the right banks, this can get you a steady stream of leads. Banks don't like turning people down, and you can become a hero from the referrals.

This has actually happened to me. My banker was visiting with someone who needed money to buy property, but the bank wasn't able to help him. The banker knew I was in the game and gave the customer my number. Before you know it, the two of us were doing a deal, and we both made money.

You can thank me when the checks start rolling in.

C. Cold call investors.

I don't know about where you live, but in my hometown, every time I drive more than three blocks, I see signs investors have put out advertising the fact that they buy houses. You know the ones I mean. They are usually simple, something along the lines of, "I buy houses," with a phone number listed on it. Other investors are also running ads on television, so they can reach as many potential deals as possible.

Good for them! They are hustling and doing what they can to build an empire. They aren't sitting back and waiting for deals to come to them. They grabbed a club, walked outside, and looked for an opportunity they could hit over the head and drag back to their cave.

Learn from these investors. Don't be passive about building your fortune as a private lender. Make things happen like they do.

The next time you see an investor's television ad or sign on the street, don't just change the channel or drive by. Write down the phone number, and call them the first chance you get.

Make your conversation short, sweet, and to the point, but let them know that you have money to lend and that you want to help them build their business.

Can you imagine how different it would be for an investor to have lenders reach out to them, instead of having to go to the bank to beg for money? Even if the investors you call don't need money at that time, I guarantee they, or someone they know, will need it in the future.

Calling investors who are making things happen is a great way to plant seeds. You don't know when you will get to harvest them, but when you do, they taste great.

Here's an actual loan I did. The individual who wanted to borrow money received my phone number from a Realtor friend of mine. This individual was also a Realtor, but he had put his license on hold. He had gotten his license thinking he would get into real estate as a Realtor.

He found out that he had inherited a property, which was a perfect prospect to flip. He figured he could earn some extra income and have a big payday; whatever his motive was, he thought he was going to hit a home run. However, he had a lot of hurdles in this acquisition.

The house may have been free, but it didn't stay that way for long. There was a mechanic's lien on the property. Just to make things interesting, back taxes were owed on the property, and the property was in disarray. This individual wanted to get into real estate fast and furious, so he borrowed from a hard moneylender who was happy to lend the cash after he saw the property.

This guy worked his tail off and kept running into one thing after another. The foundation was destroyed, and bugs were crawling everywhere. He might have crossed paths with bad contractors. This poor individual went through the ringer, trying to rehab the property and trying to make a fast profit.

His desire to make a profit was making him pull his hair out. He didn't know what else to do, and he reached out to another Realtor. He asked the Realtor if he knew anyone else who had had such a miserable experience. He needed whatever help he could find. He wanted to pursue flipping houses as a career, but he had no idea how to get the house rehabbed and on the market. The Realtor gave him my phone number and knew that I lent money. He also knew that I have written books on real estate and could help this individual in some way, maybe with a loan or maybe with some mentoring or coaching, to get him through the rehab.

The guy reached out to me, and we scheduled a meeting. I was kind of confused as to why we were meeting. He had already closed on the property, he was already rehabbing it, and, to make it worse, he was slow at communicating with me about what he wanted.

At least three times during the initial meeting, I tried to figure out how I could help. What are you asking me for? Is it advice? Is it a loan? Is it a business partnership? He couldn't articulate what was going on. He was in dire straits, and if he didn't figure things out, he was going to lose the project.

Part of the problem was that he was paying almost $2,500 in interest. He had a hard money loan with really high interest to the tune of fourteen percent. He had several signature loans. He gave a title loan on his car. He went all in on flipping a house for big profit, assuming everything would go smoothly. Unfortunately, we know life doesn't go as fast as or the way we want it to.

I felt I could help the guy out in some fashion. Here are the quick numbers. He acquired the property for free, but he had to pay about $20,000 in taxes. He got a hard money loan for $100,000, but he only withdrew $60,000 of it. I valued the property at $160,000, but he thought it would be worth $180,000.

I didn't understand what was going on. He was about ninety-five percent done on the rehab, and I couldn't understand what the problem was. Why didn’t he sell the property, take a sweet profit, and move on to the next property? It turns out he had run out of money. He burned up all of his money, and he was paying a buttload of interest. He was paying for the hard money loan, the title loan, and the signature loans. He was choking on interest.

I wanted to help him and decided that cashing out the hard money loan would be the best way to go. That's exactly what happened. I made an appointment with him to see the property, and it was gorgeous. It was definitely going to sell for $180,000, but I'm conservative, and I put my numbers down at $150,000 to $165,000.

When I walked through the property, I saw all the great work that had been done, but it needed another $5,000 to $10,000 and another month of work to be finished. I said I would be willing to knock out all his debts and pay the private lender back. He had a line of credit with the private lender, but he only exercised about $60,000, and he had a remaining balance.

To make the numbers easy, I funded a $111,000 loan. His interest on that at ten percent came out to $950 a month, and it was an interest-only loan. He was elated he was saving about $1,500 a month in interest.

That allowed him to finish the rehab and have some money left over. He could sell the property for a big profit, hopefully $60,000, and it was a win-win all the way around.

Remember that this individual was a Realtor, but he got caught on the undertow of biting off more than he could chew. He should have known better. It turned into a bigger rehab and needed bigger pockets than he had. He couldn't handle the project on his own, and that created an opportunity for me. I was able to come in and make $950 a month in interest. Talk about building your empire one deal at a time!

D. Buy existing loans.

A great way to get started as a private moneylender is to buy existing loans or refinance an investor out of the loan he currently has. A lender might have made a great deal, but his circumstances may have changed, and he might prefer to have cash now. Or, maybe he decided that being a private moneylender was no longer a good fit for his portfolio and may be looking to get out.

The advantage to you is that he has done all the hard work. He qualified the investor and the property and made sure the contractors (if any) were legit.

You may not make the same return as you would if you were in the deal from the start, but you can still make a great profit without doing all the hard work.

E. Spread the word with people you already know.

This sounds simple, but it's something I think a lot of people overlook or don't want to do.

If you are reading a book on being a private moneylender, chances are you are already investing and are savvy about it. You might even own real estate. If any of that is true, you probably know people who are investing in real estate. Some of your friends, family, or people you do business with might be flippers, wholesalers, or landlords. Let them know that The First National Bank of (insert your name here) is open and ready for business. Be sure to set up a simple one-page website, and have some business cards printed up so that you and your network can hand out your information every chance you get. Plus, you need to be active on social media and post in investor groups. If you want to make serious cash, you have to make yourself visible.

AFTER YOU FIND A BORROWER

Awesome! You hustled and found an investor who wants to pay you to borrow your money. Get ready to watch another income stream pump money into your bank account. What do you do now?

1. Get a contract or promissory note

Okay, this is another thing that sounds basic, but you might be surprised to find out a lot of people have no problem doing deals without getting everything in writing.

I hear stores about this, and they never end well. I can't wrap my mind around the fact that people actually try to do deals without a promissory note or with contracts that aren't written well enough to protect themselves. If you ever enter into a deal without a good contract, you might as well wear a T-shirt that says, "I am an idiot. Take my money, please."

Here's the stuff I have to say to protect my empire: I am not a lawyer, and you should not rely on any of this as legal advice. Before making any decisions, you should always consult a licensed professional. However, I can add a few things that I have learned and seen over my time as an investor.

There are a few things your contract must have.

A. Show me the money.

The only reason you agreed to lend money to an investor was to make money. You are allowing them to use a certain amount of your money for a certain time for a certain fee. So, what should you include? Those terms, of course. How much money are you lending? What will it be used for? When will it be paid back? How much profit will you make, or what will the interest rate be? Will there be a balloon payment at the end, or will points be applied? “Points” refers to a payment that will be made in exchange for a lower interest rate.

I have a rule. On every promissory note I sign, I require MPP, which is a mortgage, promissory note, and personal guarantee.

Another term you might explore is an exit or prepaid penalty fee, which is a set fee the borrower pays at the end of the contract’s term.

Every contract you enter into as a private moneylender should detail those things. If you are lending $100,000 for the investor to buy and rehab a house at 123 Easy Street and expect to be paid the principal amount plus $7,500 thirty days after closing, the contract needs to say that. You don’t want to leave anything to chance, and you don’t want there to be any confusion in the event things go wrong.

It may sound as if I’m focusing on the negative when I say things like this. Being a private moneylender is a great way to make money, and it's an awesome thing to add to your portfolio. If you do it right, it can give you a reliable stream of cash and help you build your empire.

One important thing to remember is that although you want to make as much money as you can, there may be limits to how much you can charge. Some lenders, who are affectionately referred to as loan sharks, charge outrageous interest rates, and this has made it almost impossible for a lot of people to pay them off. To do away with that, governments started setting limits on how much you can charge a borrower. It varies from state to state, and you need to consult with your team of professionals to make sure you don't get the local sheriff on your bad side. You don't want to get dragged into court over a few percentage points. The important thing is that you understand your rights and responsibilities, so you know what you can and cannot do.

B. Who covers the insurance and how much?

It's also a good idea to discuss the subject of insurance right from the start, and this needs to be included in your promissory note. When you act as a private lender, you are banking that the borrower has property that is worth more than the value of the loan you are offering. Your business model is to ensure that your money is guaranteed by a house or building. What happens to your money if that structure is burned down or blown away by a tornado or hurricane? Don't leave your family's future in the hands of Mother Nature. Make sure the borrower is responsible for insuring the property, so you will be protected if anything happens. You should also be listed as a loss payee.

It's good to trust people, but when it comes to business and your money, trust only goes so far. Make sure the borrower provides you with a copy of the policy and the contact information for the insurance agent who sold them the policy. Just because a clause in a contract requires someone to get insurance doesn't mean they will get it, and you want the right to make sure the insurance actually exists, and the policy will cover the property if it is damaged. Make sure you are listed as the beneficiary, so a check can't be cashed without your signature. You don't want some lowlife cashing your check and heading off to Las Vegas for a week-long blackjack vacation.

C. Get the right to monitor the progress of work on the property.

It's a bad idea to hand over a big fat check to someone and rely on them to get a deal done. I wish handshakes and honor meant something to everyone, but I, and most other investors I know, have hired people or done business with people who didn't live up to their obligations. It's sad, but the truth is that sometimes we all feel like we got screwed. One way to avoid this is to be active in the deals you do, and make sure that the work gets done.

Let's suppose you lend an investor $25,000 to rehab a house he is going to flip. He gave you the timetable for the work, and it looks as though it's going to be an easy ten percent in your pocket.

What happens if the work isn't done on time or if it never gets done? You are left holding the bag.

You can avoid this by having the right to inspect the property throughout the course of the deal. Driving over and seeing the roof is actually being replaced, or the wiring is being updated, is a foolproof and inexpensive way to make sure your investment is protected.

I'm not saying you should go over every day and armchair quarterback your investor. That might cost you deals in the future. However, you can, and should, negotiate for the right to periodically inspect the property to make sure the work is being done. Most investors would probably agree to a reasonable number of inspections, and if they object, it might be a sign that you are not dealing with the right people. You can also ask for an appraisal, so everyone has a verified number they can count on.

You should also get a scope of the work in writing. This is a simple document that explains who is going to do what. It also includes deadlines and goals. It's a great way to make sure work is being done on time. You can also require that pictures be sent, so you have visual evidence the project is moving along.

2. Vet the property.

If you are serious about lending money to an investor, you also need to vet the property. Go out and take a look at it. Take pictures, so you can review them later or show them to your contractor or investor friends who might pick up on any problems you don't see. Going out and visiting the property will give you more information than simply reading about it or hearing the investor talk about it. If the investor says nothing but good things about it, but you drive by and notice a broken sewer pipe pumping raw sewage into the basement, it is probably time to reevaluate the deal.

Get even more information by pulling up the comps on the property and ones near it. This should give you an idea of what the property is worth and whether or not you should invest in it. I also recommend drive-by appraisals. They are cheap and give you a baseline of the value.

One of the most important things to think about when being a private moneylender is location. It's an old saying, but it's true. In real estate, location can be the most import thing in determining the value of a property. Suppose an investor comes to you with a deal that looks smoking hot. You can make a great return in a short time by lending him the money to rehab a house he wants to flip. The numbers look good, but then you check the address, and something seems off. You hop in your car and drive into an area that you wouldn't want your daughter going into by herself. In the middle of a rundown neighborhood, you see the house the investor wants to sell. It looks good, and judging from the outside, it seems the investor has told you the truth.

However, the problem is that the houses surrounding it are rundown, and there is no way they will improve unless something drastic happens. If someone doesn't put some money and sweat equity into them soon, it will be too late. Those houses are an anchor on the value of your investor's property, and unless they are taken care of, the numbers the investor sent you will never add up.

It's important to remember that you should stay in your sandbox, especially when you are starting out as a private moneylender. Don't lend money on properties if you don't understand the areas where they are located. You can make money as a lender almost anywhere, but if you're used to working in Texas or Kansas, it doesn't mean you will understand what the market is like in New York or Los Angeles. The opposite is true as well. Just because you are building an empire in a big city doesn't mean you will succeed in a smaller or different market. If you are eager to pay San Francisco prices in Tulsa, you will soon be parted from your money. You will overspend and kill your budget. If you've been in the real estate game for any amount of time at all, you know you have to watch every penny. If you mess up on one part of the deal, you will be upside down for so long that your grandchildren won't even see the property make money.

Do yourself a favor. Don't invest in property if you don't understand the local market. You will save yourself a ton of headaches and a pile of cash.

3. Vet the people.

If you have read any of the other savvy investor books, you know I am a big believer in due diligence. Before you sign on the dotted line, you have to have as much information as you can get. Everything you know gives you the power to do a great deal and keeps you from losing money. Building an empire in the real estate game is hard enough. Don't make it harder on yourself by being in the dark.

Before you lend money to any investor, ask yourself, "What do I know about this guy?" Do you have any idea what kind of person she is, or are you signing a contract and handing over a check simply because it looks like a great opportunity to make money?

Here are a few ways to learn more about the people you are thinking about doing business with.

A. Have they been sued in the past over deals?

A lot of courts have websites for you to log in and enter someone's name. In a minute or so, you can see if they have been sued or if they are in the habit of suing people. It's great information to have, but it's important to take this information with a grain of salt.

Remember that we live in a very litigious society. People like to sue over almost anything, and if you have been in business for longer than a month, you may have been sued, too. Any knucklehead with filing fees (sometimes these are less than

$100) can run down to the courthouse and sue somebody because they think they have been wronged. Many business owners consider lawsuits a cost of doing business, and they expect to be sued even if they don't deserve to be. If you haven't been sued, don't worry, you will be. It's just a matter of time.

If your investor has been sued a few times, it wouldn't necessarily raise a red flag for me, especially if he has been in the game for a while. However, if he has only done four deals and has been sued three times (and lost every case), that might be an issue for me. If it looks like a great deal, and the investor seems like someone I might want to do business with, I might ask a few questions for clarification.

The point is to do your due diligence. It's the only way to cover yourself.

"Don't take the casual approach to life. Casualness leads to casualties."

–JIM ROHN

B. Ask for references.

Another great way to qualify investors is to ask them for references. If they have been doing deals for a while, they can give you the names of people who can vouch for their ability to get deals done and make money. If they can't, I wouldn't be too worried, especially if they are new to real estate. If they can, it is a great way to protect your money and make sure you are doing business with the right people.

Remember, your loan is backed by collateral, and that is the most important part of MPP.

C. Ask for tax returns or bank statements.

As you probably know, a lot of people talk. They can go on and on about all the things they are going to do one day. Some of them even tell stories about things they have done, none of which are true.

A few people actually take action. They put down the remote control, get off the couch, go outside, and get stuff done. They hustle and do what they have to do to build their empires. These are my people, and if you are serious about making things happen, you know what I mean.

As a private moneylender, the key is to separate the wannabes from the people who really want to make money. You don't want to waste time or get into a deal that is doomed to fail because the investor you agreed to help isn't serious or able to get the deal done.

Asking for tax returns or bank statements is a great way to make sure you are doing business with doers, not talkers. If someone tells you she has done five deals in the past two years, looking at her financial documents is a great way to verify she is being upfront and honest with you.

It's also good to remember that you need to be honest with investors who want to borrow money. Don't be afraid to let someone know if it's your first deal or that you have only done a few deals. If you are dealing with the right people, they won't put up with you being dishonest any more than you would if they lied to you. Be transparent, and your bank account will thank you.

While you are vetting the investor, you can also vet their contractors the same way. The wrong contractor can screw things up not only by doing crappy work, but also by failing to pay for supplies. In many places, if a contractor buys material on credit, uses them on a house, but fails to pay for the material, the vendor can place a lien on the property. Make sure your money is going to people who do things the right way, so you don't lose sleep wondering if a materials lien is going to screw things up when your investor tries to sell the property.

4. Vet the appraisal.

When investors come to you to with deals, some will come with appraisals in hand. It would be hard for many lenders to consider a deal if they didn't know what the property was worth. The truth is that all appraisals are not created equal. Depending on when the appraisal was done and who did it, there can be a big difference on the value of a property. Suppose a house was appraised two months before property values crashed. The appraisal may have been fair at the time, but if the same house was appraised six months later when property values dropped to their lowest values in decades, you would see a very different number.

The same house could be appraised at different values by different appraisers, even if they do them at the same time. What if you knew that the appraiser on your investor's house was married to the investor's sister? Do you think that might have an impact on the numbers he might send back?

The point is that you shouldn't rely only on an appraisal to determine the value of a property. Get as much information as you can from as many sources as possible, so you have the power to make the right deals.

5. Create a paper trail wherever you go.

This should be part of your company's logo. Maybe you should have it tattooed on your forehead, so you can see it every morning when you look in the mirror. Never do anything without a way to document it. If you don't document, it will cost you money and time in the future.

Let's suppose you lend an investor $25,000 to buy a property. You've done business with him before and don't feel the need for a contract. You do the deal on a handshake, and everything goes well. You visit the property, see the work is being done, and sleep well at night, confident you made a good deal. Your empire is growing, just as you planned.

The night before the closing, your investor is killed by a drunk driver. His brother, a guy you have never met, is appointed administer of his estate. When you call him about closing the deal and sending you a check, he asks, "Where's the agreement? I'd be happy to pay you as soon as I see something with my brother's signature on it." How likely is it you will be paid for your handshake deal?

Creating a paper trail solves a lot of problems, and it makes it easier for judges to rule in your favor if, or when, you get dragged into court. It's also a great way to keep the IRS off your back, but I'm sure that thought doesn't bother you.

Make life simple by creating a paper trail that covers your butt.

Q&A

1. Do you need to have a license or register to be a private lender?

The short answer is no. In 2008, the federal government passed The Secure and Fair Enforcement for Mortgage Licensing Act. It states that lenders are required to have a license if they meet certain criteria. Those criteria are: 1) the lender originates the loan; and 2) the loan is secured with one- to four-family (fourplex) residences in real estate. Known today as The SAFE Act, this regulation requires these lenders to adhere to national standards for lending. It also requires state-licensed lenders to take classes, pass a licensing exam, and complete background checks. Most of us will never meet those standards, so rock on, player.

2. If I run out of money and my aunt lets me rent out her money, can I broker her money to an investor?

Yes! Hit up Aunt Millie for some cash, and lend it out to as many investors as you can. Just make sure you pay her back. You don't want her going old school on you with her walker. They don't play at the old folks' home when it comes to money. And no, you don't have to have a license for that.

3. I just found a lender who wants to borrow some money. Should I ask for references before I give him the check?

You should only ask for references if you are interested in being paid back. If you want to be played, lend money to whoever asks you for it, and don't ask any questions. Due diligence is the key if you want to build an empire. Vet everyone. You might even vet the reference. You can also call them just to make sure everything is on the up-and-up. The more due diligence you have upfront, the fewer headaches you will have in the future. It won't eliminate the headaches, but it will prevent a good many of them.

4. What's a good interest rate to charge?

I wish I could tell you to charge whatever you can negotiate, but it's not that simple. The range is six to twelve percent, and the average seems to be ten. Before you lend any money, make sure to check local laws. Most states have usury laws that limit the amount of interest you can charge. If you charge too much, you may find yourself on the wrong end of a lawsuit or arrest warrant. Know the limits, and get every penny you can.

5. What's a reasonable origination fee or points to charge?

One percent is what I usually see, and I have a lot of experience lending and borrowing money. However, I've also seen deals with no fee. It depends on the size of the loan and the relationship between the parties. There is no standard; it's all a negotiation.

6. Should I charge fees like a documentation fee, wire fee, or rubber stamp fee?

Charge whatever you can, player. As long as you are open and honest about the fees, and there are no laws prohibiting them, knock yourself out. Maybe you could even make up a few. How about a "lender had to come in on Thursday" fee or "I froze my butt off lending money in January" fee?

For those less adventurous types who want to stick with the tried and true, a typical documentation fee in my area is $250, but there could be attorney fees involved as well. It depends on the circumstances.

7. How do you calculate after-repair value (ARV) on a property?

Typically, you add the purchase price and any repairs that were done to get the property ready for sale or lease. That sounds simple, but other factors come into play when determining ARV. The type of market, such as low-margin housing, can affect how ARV is calculated. Another example or issue is whether or not closing fees are included in ARV calculations.

The main points are to understand exactly how the lender calculates this crucial number and to make sure it aligns with your profit goals for your investment.

8. If I'm lending money on a deal, should I require the borrower to make a down payment?

Sometimes. It depends on the quality of the collateral. If you lend fifty percent on an asset, you don't need to require a down payment. However, if a deal is skinny, or the borrower is a rookie, it may make sense to charge one. Everybody needs to have skin in the game. Requiring a down payment is a simple way to make sure everyone takes the matter seriously.

9. How do I file a lien or mortgage or make this process official?

Good question. Ideas like this are what separate newbies from veterans. This varies by state, but the general idea is you have to file it with the state or county to make it official. It's important to understand how this is done because once the lien is on file, it puts everyone on notice that the property is secured. Guess what would happen if you didn't file your lien? Some scumbag borrower you thought you could trust would mortgage the same property fifteen times, and no one would know until it hit the fan. Then it would be too late because you and lot of other suckers would be down at the county courthouse trying to be first in line to get something. Make sure each and every deal is secured by a properly file lien. A great quick fix is to use a title or escrow company. They will make sure your interests are protected.

10. Should I do a bridge loan, and how should I charge for that?

Bridge loans, which are temporary loans to cover someone, usually for a short period, can be a great way to make money. It's another brick you can use to build your empire. What to charge depends on the borrower, the asset, and how long the borrower needs the money. Charge a flat fee or percentage, both of which can be negotiated.

11. I'm getting ready to lend private money to an investor. Should I pull his credit?

Most private lenders don't, but do whatever makes you feel comfortable. If you set things up correctly, you will be lending on an asset, not a person. Your deal should be secured by a mortgage and lien, or something similar, so you are guaranteed to get your money from the deal. However, if you still feel uncomfortable, you should see a copy of the borrower's credit history for peace of mind.

12. I feel comfortable enough to lend someone money. What are the next steps?

Way to go, rock star! You're crushing it! Here's what you need to do to take your empire to the next level.

1. Find an investor who needs to borrow your money. We talked about this earlier in the book, but to reiterate, networking is the best way to find investors who are looking for lenders. A few great ways to network include:
    a. Attending real estate events and clubs.
    b. Cold calling investors who have "We Buy Houses" signs posted around town.
    c. Developing relationships with bankers.
    d. Spreading the word with people you already know.
    e. Setting up a simple website.
    f. Printing up and passing out business cards.
2. Have prospective borrowers fill out a simple application that gives you information you can vet. Although the law is clear that you should lend to an LLC and not an individual, it never hurts to know about the people you are doing business with. The application should have at least the following basic information:
    a. First, middle, and last names
    b. Personal address of the prospect

c. Business name and address
d. Tax identification number of the business
e. Social security number of the owner or managing member
f. Phone number and email address
g. Loan amount requested
h. Desired terms
i. Collateral property address
j. Estimated repair costs
k. Intention of the prospect in regards to the property (i.e., buy-and-hold, flip, etc.)
l. At least three business references

3. Vet the information

Prospects:

a. Use your state's court network to search the prospect's name. Oklahoma's court network is OSCN, and it allows you to see court cases filed by or against your prospect. You are looking for lawsuits pertaining to collections, fraudulent business deals, or excessive lawsuits filed by the prospect. If you find any of these types of filings, you might want to rethink lending to this prospect.
b. Call the business references, and have a candid conversation regarding the prospect's character and integrity.

Property:

a. Conduct an internet search on the property. This will allow you to get a general idea of the value of the property. You may even find pictures of the property that will help you determine if the property will be a worthy asset.
b. Conduct research on the neighborhood where the property is located. This is an important factor in determining the actual value or salability of the property.

If you are still interested in lending the money after doing all these things, ask the prospect for an appraisal, and physically go to the property to ensure the pictures you saw on Google are an accurate depiction of the property, and the neighborhood doesn't tank the value.

13. Are you able to walk me through the loan process?

Sure. I got you.

Once you've agreed on the loan amount and terms, you are ready to start the paperwork. A precursor to starting the paperwork is getting all the needed identification documents from the prospect. You will need a copy of a state-issued identification card and a social security card. You will also need a certificate of good standing for their business. Investors normally do business as a limited liability company (LLC). This certificate shows that their LLC is still active. If you require financial information from your prospect, you will also need these documents before you start the contract process.

Documents can be found on numerous websites. My suggestion is to use the website documents as a template. Modify what you find on the internet to suit your needs. Once the documents are created to your satisfaction, spend the money to have an attorney review them. This is a *must*. You will only have to do this the first time you create them. Once created and validated by an attorney, you can use the same documents for all future loans. Spending the money up front can save you a ton of time and money in the future.

1. Mortgage:
   The mortgage is the legal document that assigns the property as collateral on the loan.
2. Promissory note:
   The promissory note stipulates the size of the debt, its interest rate, and late fees. In this case, the lender holds the promissory note until the mortgage loan is paid off.
3. Personal guarantee:
   This is the individual's legal promise to repay the loan issued to a business for which they serve as an executive or partner. This will allow you to hold the individual, as well as the business, liable should there be a default on the loan.

14. I am a little timid about lending money. Am I missing something?

I get it. Private lending isn't for everyone, but if you understand it, you might see it's a great way to turn a little bit of money into a lot of money. That's the thought that gets investors out of bed in the morning, isn't it? There are certainly risks with private lending, but if you do it right, it's an awesome way to add passive income to your portfolio.

There are a lot of great reasons to be a private investor, including:

a. Building a retirement account.
b. Having a reliable second income.
c. Using your IRA funds to generate higher returns.
d. Increasing your returns by diversifying your investment portfolio.
e. Generating income to cover living expenses after you retire.
f. Cashing in on the great returns real estate offers without having to be a landlord.
g. Investing in assets that are less volatile than the stock market.
h. Putting an unexpected inheritance to use.

I bet at least one of these ideas appeals to you. Take the plunge. Being a private moneylender is a great way to make your money work for you. Ask around. I'm sure at least one member of your local investors' club is lending money. Don't let them have all the fun and make all the money.

15. I forgot everything I knew about lending ratios. Are you able to tell me again?

Here are three of the most common lending ratios you will need:

1. Loan-to-value (LTV):

   You lend a percentage of the current as-is value of the property. This might be higher than the purchase price if the borrower is buying the property at a big discount.

2. After-repair value (ARV):

   You lend money based on the ARV. It is the future projection of the property value, assuming the borrower completes any rehab work. If you do loan-to-value (ARV), your investment is seen as a percentage of the future value of the property.

3. Loan-to-contract:

   You lend money based on a purchase price stated in the purchase contract. If the loan-to-contract ratio is less than 100 percent, the borrower will need more money to complete the purchase, as well as any planned repairs or rehab.

16. Should I lend money other than on real estate?

Yes, but only if you want to make money. I lend money to people in the craziest ways. This includes lending $1,000 to a Realtor friend and $3,000 to someone who offices out of one of my commercial properties.

Microloans like that are considered signatures loans in my world. The biggest benefit of these is creating goodwill and relationships by helping people when they need it. Don't get in the habit of lending on unsecured loans, or you may lose your shirt. Only lend money you are willing to lose.

17. What are good basic borrower criteria?

Ideally, you should work with someone who has been in real estate for a while. If you get lucky, they may know more than you on things such as paperwork. It's important you feel comfortable with them because making a good deal happen is a team effort. You want someone with a track record, someone who has been hustling and slugging it out on the street. I'm not a fan of lending money to first-time borrowers, but under the right circumstances, it can end up being a sweet deal. Regardless of who you work with, make sure you have a firm deal and an enforceable contract.

18. How do I know this borrower will pay me back instead of taking a family vacation? What should I do if I see sketchy behavior?

Here are some early-stage red flags I look out for that might indicate your borrower could end up being a problem if things go wrong:

a. They have no cash reserves.
b. To save money, they want to do the rehab themselves or hire their brother-in-law who is not a general contractor.
c. They don't respond to you in a timely manner.
d. You ask specific questions but only get vague answers in return.
e. They tell you there is no risk to the investment.
f. They don't provide any documentation about the project or their work on it.
g. They have no exit plan for the investment.
h. They don't have much experience on the type of investment they are trying to borrow money for.
i. Their timelines for the project are overly optimistic.
j. They don't have a good team of people around them.
k. Your gut tells you something is off.

Sometimes, it may just be a matter of style. If your working style doesn't gel with a borrower's style, it might be best to pass on the deal. You don't want to get stuck working with the wrong people. No amount of money will make that worth your while. Always remember you are in the driver's seat. There are plenty of great borrowers out there seeking private funding for their deals.

19. How do I close a private loan?

The best and simplest way is to use a title and escrow company or an attorney to close any loan you originate. Be sure you have full title work completed, and get lender's title insurance. Most importantly, require the borrower to pay for it.

The Golden Rule, the one that must never be broken, is that you never, *ever*, send money to your borrower directly. Always send it to title or closing company, so they can file a lien on the property and protect your investment.

ONE NAGGING THOUGHT

So, you've read the book and are ready to kick butt and take names as a private lender, but you have one thought you can't get rid of: What happens if your borrower defaults on a private money loan?

This is rare, and I hope it never happens to you. It's easier for everyone if all parties live up to their end of the deal. However, life s+ometimes gets in the way, and if a borrower defaults on a loan, it can still have a positive ending for all parties involved.

Let's recap what should happen if you have done the right things as a private moneylender. You should be sitting in a good position because you lent seventy percent value of the asset (property), so if it has to be sold, your loan will be covered. You may even have a gain in this position. Depending on the amount of your loan and the value of the property, you could make more on a default than you would if the loan had been paid. I'm not wishing anyone any harm, but if a borrower defaults, it doesn't bother me if it puts more cash in my pocket.

Let's break down the steps to take if a borrower defaults. These are general steps, and each state might have its own requirements, so you need to check with your attorney to make sure everything is done the way your state needs it to be done.

First, you have to give them notice of default. You need to send them a letter stating how much they owe and what will happen if they don't get their papers straight. It should probably be sent by certified mail, so you can create a paper trail.

Second, you need to file paperwork with the county courthouse. It has to be done a certain way, so you need to be familiar with that process. You can have an attorney do this for you if you are willing to pay for it, and you might be able to have them do it with one simple phone call.

Third, after the process makes its way through the court system, you will own the asset outright.

Fourth, list the asset for sale with a Realtor.

Fifth, sit back and wait for the funds from the sale to hit your bank account. If you ran the numbers right on the front end, you should have a greater return than you would have expected. This thought crosses my mind when I lend money to investors. Again, I'm not hoping anyone defaults, but it's awesome to know that I'm protected if things don't go the way they are supposed to.

This process is super simple, and anyone can do it. The hardest part is getting over the mental hurdles and disappointment that someone didn't perform as expected.

Another savvy way to deal with this is to have the lender sign a deed in lieu of foreclosure. This is an agreement where a borrower in default voluntarily turns over ownership of a property to the lender to avoid the foreclosure process. A deed in lieu of foreclosure might also keep you from facing personal liability for any outstanding balance on the mortgage. It can be a win-win for everyone. Sometimes this is called "cash for keys."

CONCLUSION

So, there it is. Private money lending is a great way to help build your empire. It's a proven way to use your money to create a passive revenue stream.

You don't have to be a rocket scientist to do this, but you do have to follow a few rules and make sure you cover your butt.

The only question you should be asking at this point is, "Why shouldn't I be a private moneylender?" Maybe you don't like money, or maybe you don't want to make more. I doubt that's the case because if you believed either of those things, you wouldn't have picked up this book.

If you do your homework and cover your bases, there aren't many reasons you shouldn't be a private moneylender. Get your money out of the stock market or your IRA, and start earning some real returns. Be savvy, and use that cash to build an empire to give your family the lives they deserve.

See you at the next level, baller.

TERMS

401k: A retirement savings plan funded by employees and often matched by contributions from the employer; contributions are usually made before taxes and grow tax-free until withdrawn, although after-tax contributions are also allowed.

529 plan: A savings plan operated by a state or educational institution designed to help set aside funds for future college costs. Savings deposited in a 529 plan grow tax-free until withdrawn.

Absentee owner: An individual or group that owns a property without occupying it or participating in the management of the property's day-to-day needs.

Accrued interest: Interest that has been earned but not yet received.

Actuarial assumption: Estimate made for the purpose of an actuarial valuation. Possible variables include life expectancy, return on investments, interest rates, and growth in earnings.

Adjustable-rate mortgage (ARM): Mortgage loan for which the interest rate is raised or lowered periodically in accordance with a stated reference interest rate. ARM refers both to the original homeowner loan and to a securitized pool of such loans.

After-repair value (ARV): The estimated value of a property after completed renovations, not in its current condition. House flippers commonly use ARV as a way to gauge the worth of a fixer-upper property, including how much it can be bought, and then resold, for after repairs.

Agency broker: Broker/dealer who acts as an agent between market makers and investors.

Amortization (AM): Repayment by installments over a period of time.

Annual fee: A yearly fee associated with some financial accounts.

Annual percentage rate (APR): Cost of debt that is paid by borrowers, expressed as an annualized figure.

Annuity: Contract designed to provide regular payments to the policyholder in return for an initial lump sum payment. Annuities may have a guaranteed period and/or be payable for life. Payments may be fixed or may vary.

Appraisal: A real estate appraisal, property valuation, or land valuation is the process of developing an opinion of value for real property. Real estate transactions often require appraisals because they occur infrequently, and every property is unique.

Arbitrage: An investment strategy for which an investor simultaneously buys and sells an asset in different markets to take advantage of a price difference and to help generate a profit. While price differences are typically small and short-lived, the returns can be impressive when multiplied by a large volume.

Asking price: The price a seller states they will accept. The seller may qualify the stated asking price as firm or negotiable. Firm means the seller is implying that the price is fixed and will not change.

Asset allocation: Asset allocation is an investment strategy that aims to balance risk and reward by apportioning a portfolio's assets according to an individual's goals, risk tolerance, and investment horizon.

Asset class: Broad category of assets of a similar type. Examples include equities, bonds, property, and cash.

Asset swap: The exchange of a flow of payments from a given security (the asset) in return for a different set of cash flows.

Asset-backed security (ABS): A type of financial investment that is collateralized by an underlying pool of assets—usually ones that generate cash flow from debt, such as loans, leases, credit card balances, or receivables. It takes the form of a bond or note, paying income at a fixed rate for a set amount of time until maturity. For income-oriented investors, asset-backed securities can be an alternative to other debt instruments, such as corporate bonds or bond funds.

Asset: Anything that has a monetary value.

Audit: Unbiased examination and opinion of the financial statements of an organization. It can be internal (by employees of the organization) or external (by an outside firm).

Bad debt: Debt which is viewed as unlikely to be recovered by the creditor and may be written off as worthless.

Balance: The amount of money in a savings or checking account, or the amount of money owed on a credit card account.

Baller: A lavishly successful person. The term can also describe someone or something as "excellent," especially in some spectacular way.

Bankruptcy: Legally declared state that is usually triggered by a company's failure or impaired ability to meet its contractual debt obligations. Bankruptcy usually results in restructuring the company's debt or in liquidation of the company.

Bargain: Another word for transaction or deal. It does not imply that a particularly favorable price was obtained.

Base rate (prime rate): Benchmark for other interest rates, including personal loans and mortgages.

Basis Point: 1/100 of 1%, or 0.01%, thus 100bp = 1%.

Beneficial owner: Person who enjoys the benefits deriving from a security or property. May be different from the legal owner in whose name the title is registered.

Bitcoin: A type of digital currency for which a record of transactions is maintained, and new units of currency are generated by the computational solution of mathematical problems, and which operates independently of a central bank.

Blue chip stocks: A huge company with an excellent reputation. These are typically large, well-established, and financially sound companies that have operated for many years and that have dependable earnings, often paying dividends to investors.

Book value: Value at which a security is recorded on a balance sheet, usually the cost of buying it.

Bookkeeping: The recording of financial transactions and exchanges.

Boom: Period of rapid economic growth.

Bridge loan: A type of short-term loan, typically taken out for a period of two weeks to three years pending the arrangement of larger or longer-term financing.

Broker/dealer: Individual or firm that acts as an intermediary between buyers and sellers, usually for a payment of commission.

Build to suit: A type of real estate transaction where a property owner or developer will construct a building for sale or lease that will be built to the tenant's or buyer's specifications.

Buy-and-hold: A long-term real estate investment strategy where a real estate investor buys an investment property with the intent to hold the asset for the considerable future. Along the way, the investor can earn passive income through the rental income on the property and use this cash flow to pay the mortgage.

Capital gains tax (CGT): Tax levied on the sale of an asset, based on the increase in its price since purchase.

Capital gains: Profits from the sale of an investment.

Capital growth: The value of an asset or investment over time. Capital growth is measured by the difference between the current value, or market value, of an asset or investment and its purchase price, or the value of the asset or investment at the time it was acquired.

Capital: Wealth in the form of money or property.

Cash flow: The total amount of money being transferred into or out of a business, account, or individual budget.

Cash flow: When it comes to rental property investing, your "cash flow" is the net amount of money that piles up in or disappears from your bank account each month.

Cash reserves: The money a company or individual keeps on hand to meet short-term and emergency funding needs.

Caveat emptor: The principle that a buyer is responsible for checking the quality and suitability of goods before making a purchase. Latin phrase for "let the buyer beware."

Certificate of deposit (CD): A certificate issued by a bank to a person depositing money for a specified length of time.

Cha-ching: The sound a cash register makes, used as an exclamation.

Charitable contributions: Cash, stocks, gifts, or other items donated to a charitable organization.

Charitable giving: The act of giving money or other items to a nonprofit, charitable organization.

Chief executive officer (CEO): The highest ranking person in a company.

Chief financial officer (CFO): The top financial position in an organization. This position is responsible for tracking cash flow and financial planning, as well as analyzing the company's financial strengths and weaknesses and proposing strategic directions.

Collateral: Property or assets that are committed by an individual in order to guarantee a loan. Upon default, the collateral becomes subject to seizure by the lender and may be sold to satisfy the debt.

Collateralized debt obligation (CDO): A complex structured finance product that is backed by a pool of loans and other assets. These underlying assets serve as collateral if the loan goes into default. Though risky and not for all investors, CDOs are a viable tool for shifting risk and freeing up capital.

Commercial mortgage-backed security (CMBS): Mortgage-backed security collateralized by commercial rather than residential mortgage loans. Unlike residential MBSs, CMBSs are not usually subject to prepayment risk, as most underlying loans do not permit prepayment without substantial penalties

Commercial paper: A short-term debt instrument used by corporations to finance borrowing needs. This means these debt obligations aren't backed by any specific collateral. As an everyday example, a mortgage is a form of secured debt as it's backed by the value of the underlying real estate.

Commercial real estate (CRE): Buildings and land that are intended for profit-generating activities, rather than regular residential purposes.

Commission: Payments made directly to real estate brokers for services rendered in the sale or purchase of property. A commission is usually a percentage of the property's selling price, though it can also be a flat fee.

Comparable (comps): A real estate appraisal term referring to properties with characteristics that are like a subject property for which the value is being sought.

Construction lien: A claim made against a property by a contractor or subcontractor who has not been paid for work done on that property.

Credit rating: A financial institution's evaluation of an individual's ability to manage debt.

Credit report: A document outlining an individual's credit history, for use by credit card issuers and others considering providing a person with a loan.

Credit reporting agency: A company that compiles and provides information to creditors to facilitate their decisions about extending credit.

Credit score: A number representing a person's creditworthiness, based on past credit and payment history.

Creditor: A person or business to whom money is owed.

Creditworthiness: An analysis made by a lender about a consumer's riskiness as a borrower.

Crunching the numbers: The act of processing numerical data.

Crushing it: An expression used when someone is doing their job particularly well or exceeding all of their goals.

Cryptocurrency: A digital currency for which transactions are verified and records maintained by a decentralized system using cryptography, rather than by a centralized authority.

Debt collectors: Businesses or individuals that pursue the payment of debts owed.

Debt consolidation: Taking out one loan to cover a variety of debts, often with the goal of paying a lower overall interest rate.

Debt: The state of owing money to another individual or business, or the amount of money borrowed.

Depreciation: The decrease in value of assets over time.

Direct mail campaign: Also known as direct mail, junk mail, mailshot, admail, letterbox drop, or letterboxing, it is the delivery of advertising material to recipients via postal mail.

Diversify or diversification: A risk management strategy that mixes a wide variety of investments within a portfolio. A diversified portfolio contains a mix of distinct asset types and investment vehicles in an attempt at limiting exposure to any single asset or risk.

Dividend: A sum paid regularly by a company to its shareholders.

Document fees: Document preparation or doc fee is to prepare the deed to legally transfer title from the seller to the buyer or, in this case, from the borrower to the lender.

Down payment: The amount a consumer pays up front for something on the day of the purchase.

Drive-by appraisal: A drive-by appraisal, also referred to as a summary appraisal, is an alternative form of home appraisal. Instead of inspecting both the interior and exterior, the appraiser only needs to examine the exterior of the property and any available real estate records to determine the home's value

Due diligence: The investigation or exercise of care that a reasonable business or person is normally expected to take before entering into an agreement or contract with another party.

Emergency fund: Money set aside for emergency expenses, recommended to cover six to nine months' worth of living costs.

Entrepreneur: Someone who owns or operates his or her own business.

Equal Credit Opportunity Act: A law that helps to protect consumers from being discriminated against due to race, sex, marital status, religion, or age when obtaining credit.

Equity: The value of a homeowner's interest in the home; the actual property's current market value, less any liens that are attached to that property.

Estate: The whole of an individual's possessions, including property and debts.

Expenditures: The action of spending funds or an amount of money spent.

Expense: The money an individual regularly spends for items or services.

Finance: To borrow funds for the purpose of a purchase.

Financial advisor: A professional who provides financial services and advice to individuals or businesses.

Financial partnership: A relationship that requires financial dependence, contribution, and communication.

Financial plan: A strategy for handling one's finances to ensure the greatest future benefit.

Fixed expenses: Expenses that are the same each month.

Fixed-rate mortgage: An installment loan that has a fixed interest rate for the entire term of the loan.

Flat rate: A rate that does not vary with usage or time of use.

Flipping houses: Purchasing an asset and holding it for only a short period of time before reselling it.

Foreclosure: A legal process for which a mortgaged property is taken because the borrower has failed to keep up on payments.

General contractor (GC): A general contractor, main contractor, or prime contractor is responsible for the day-to-day oversight of a construction site, management of vendors and trades, and the communication of information to all involved parties throughout the course of a building project.

Good debt: The concept that sometimes it is worth taking on certain types of debt in order to generate income in the long run. Two common examples include college education debt and real estate.

Grace period: The time a borrower is allowed after a payment is due to make that payment without adding to the interest owed.

Gross income: The total amount of money an individual has earned before taxes are taken out.

Guaranteed interest rate: The minimum interest rate an investor can expect from an issuing company.

Hard money: A specific type of asset-based loan financing through which a borrower receives funds secured by real property.

Health savings account (HSA): A pre-tax savings account designed specifically for medical expenses.

HELOC: A home equity line of credit.

HUD: Also known as a closing statement, a HUD is a standardized mortgage lending form in use in the United States of America on which creditors or their closing agents itemize all charges imposed on buyers and sellers in consumer credit mortgage transactions.

Income tax: Tax levied by a government directly on personal income.

Income: Payment received for goods or services, including employment.

Individual retirement account fund (IRA): A retirement account that allows individuals to contribute a limited yearly sum toward retirement on either a pre-tax (traditional IRA) or after-tax (Roth IRA) basis.

Inflation: The overall increase in the cost of products and services over time.

Interest rate: The rate at which a borrower pays interest for borrowing an item or money or the percentage rate earned on a given investment.

Invest: To expend money with the expectation of earning a profit on that fund over time.

Investment strategy: A set of rules or procedures to guide an investor's selections.

Investment: An item or financial product on which a consumer expects to earn a profit in the future.

Investment portfolio: A range of investments held by a person or organization.

Lease: A contract outlining the rental terms of a piece of property, whether it is a car, an apartment, or another space.

Letter of intent: A document declaring the preliminary commitment of one party to do business with another. The letter outlines the chief terms of a prospective deal.

Leveraging: Any technique involving borrowing funds to buy things, hoping that future profits will be many times more than the cost of borrowing.

Limited liability company (LLC): A business structure in the US that protects its owners from personal responsibility for its debts or liabilities.

Loan principal: An amount borrowed that remains unpaid, excluding interest.

Loan term: The period of time during which a loan is active.

Loan-to-cost ratio (LTC): The loan amount divided by the construction cost.

Loan-to-value ratio (LTV): A comparison between the loan amount and the expected market value of a completed project.

Loan: Money or assets borrowed and paid back with interest over time.

Long-term financial goal: A financial goal that will take longer than a year to achieve.

Low-margin housing: The selling price chosen for a house isn't much higher than its cost.

Market value: The amount for which something can be sold in a given market.

Maximum allowable offer (MAO): A tried-and-true calculation real estate investors use to determine the price they would like to offer on a particular investment property. It is an equation that ensures investors maintain the desired profit, while also considering expected fixed and rehab costs.

Maximum purchase price (MPP): Making this calculation requires the following five steps:

Step 1) Determine gross operating income (GOI): This is done by taking gross scheduled income and subtracting an amount for vacancy and credit loss. Gross scheduled income is all the income you would receive from rents if all the units were rented.

- Gross scheduled income - vacancy allowance and credit loss = gross operating income

Step 2) Determine net operating income (NOI): This is accomplished by subtracting operating expenses from gross operating income. Operating expenses are expenses required to keep the property in service (i.e., property taxes, insurance, utilities, etc.).

- Gross operating income - operating expenses = net operating income

Step 3) Compute net income percentage (NIP): This is achieved by dividing net operating income by gross operating income.

Net operating income ÷ gross operating income = net income percentage

Step 4) Compute down payment percentage (DPP): In this case, you'll need to know the average gross rent multiplier (GRM) in your area and the current market interest rate (I).

- (Net income percentage ÷ (GRM x I)) - 1 = down payment percentage

Step 5) Compute maximum purchase price (MPP): This allows you to discover how much you can afford to pay to break even.

- Available down payment ÷ down payment percentage = maximum purchase price

Example:

Say you have $75,000 to invest and want to determine the maximum purchase price you can pay for the investment property without going below a break-even cash flow. We'll assume that you conducted both a market study and financial analysis (steps one and two above) and arrived at the following numbers:

Gross operating income: $10,000
Net operating income: $7,500
Gross rent multiplier: 10.0

Current interest rate: 6%

First, calculate the net income percentage (NIP): 7,500 ÷ 10,000 = 75%

Next, calculate the down payment percentage (DPP): (.75 ÷ (10 x .06)) - 1 = .25

Finally, calculate the maximum purchase price (MPP) $75,000 ÷ .25 = $300,000

Mechanic's lien: A legal guarantee of payment to builders, contractors, and subcontractors for the building or renovation of a property.

Medium-term financial goal: A financial goal that will require less than a year to achieve.

Mentor: An experienced and trusted adviser.

Mortgage: A loan secured in order to purchase property. It allows you to borrow money to purchase or refinance a home and gives the lender the right to take your property if you fail to repay the money you've borrowed.

Mortgage loan: A loan for the purpose of purchasing real estate.

Mortgage payment: The payment a borrower makes each month toward the purchase of a home.

Mortgage term: The agreed upon amount of time to pay off a mortgage.

Multiple listing service (MLS): Private databases that are created, maintained, and paid for by real estate professionals to help their clients buy and sell property.

Mutual fund: An investment program funded by shareholders that trades in diversified holdings and is professionally managed.

Networking: The action or process of interacting with others to exchange information and develop professional or social contacts.

New York Stock Exchange (NYSE): A stock exchange located in New York City that is the largest equities-based exchange in the world, based on the total market capitalization of its listed securities.

Nonprofit organization: An organization chartered for purposes other than making profits.

Off market: In real estate, "off market" can mean two things: a home is not for sale, or it's for sale but not listed. Most generally, "off market" means that a property wasn't listed on the MLS by an agent. The MLS doesn't hold all the properties that are for sale.

Opportunity cost: The difference between any profit actually earned and the profit that could have been earned. Let's say the investor earned a five percent profit on the actual investment

(Opportunity "A") but could have earned ten percent on the investment opportunity not chosen (Opportunity "B").

Origination fee: A mortgage origination fee is a fee charged by the lender in exchange for processing a loan. It is typically a percentage of the total loan amount.

Paper trail: A series of documents providing written evidence of a sequence of events or the activities of a person or organization.

Passive investing: An investment strategy to maximize returns on a recurring basis with little or no effort on the part of the investor.

Personal guaranty: An individual's legal promise to repay credit issued to a business for which they serve as an executive or partner.

Personal property insurance: Personal property is the stuff you own, such as furniture, electronics, and clothing. Whether you own a home or rent an apartment, insurance policies typically include personal property coverage. This type of coverage helps pay to repair or replace your belongings after a covered loss, such as theft or fire.

Points: Fees a homebuyer pays directly to the lender in exchange for a reduced interest rate.

Portfolio: A collection of real estate investment assets and/or a comprehensive document that details your past and present real estate investment assets. You can think of it as similar to a resume.

Private mortgage insurance (PMI): Insurance to help protect a mortgage lender in the event a borrower cannot make payments.

Promissory note: A signed document containing a written promise to pay a stated sum to a specified person or bearer at a specified date or on demand.

Property tax: A capital tax on property based on its estimated value.

Purchase price: The price paid for an item or service.

Purchasing power: The financial ability to buy products and services.

Real Estate Investors Associations (REIA): A trade organization for real estate investors. The purpose of REIA is to provide networking opportunities and educational events, to advocate on behalf of the industry, to help members connect with the local community, and to bring buying power to the members in the form of local and national discounts. REIAs range from small, informal groups to more organized and larger groups with hundreds or even thousands of members.

Recession: A period of economic decline during which trade and industrial activity are reduced.

Refinance: To finance something again, typically with a new loan at a lower rate of interest

Rehab: A real estate rehab is when investors purchase a property, complete renovations, and sell it for a profit or use it as a rental. These projects can take anywhere from a few weeks to a few months, depending on the amount of work needed.

Renovations: The process of improving a broken, damaged, or outdated structure. Renovations are typically either commercial or residential. Additionally, renovation can refer to making something new or bringing something back to life and can apply in social contexts.

Resale value: The amount at which an individual or company would be able to sell a specific item.

Residential real estate: An area developed for people to live in as defined by local zoning ordinances.

Return on investment (ROI): Also known as the rate of return (ROR), this is the profit one makes on an investment.

Risk: The possibility of financial loss.

Securitized loan: A loan that is protected by collateral to ensure loan repayment.

Self-directed IRA: A type of IRA managed by the account owner that can hold a variety of alternative investments.

Shareholder: An individual or legal entity that is registered by the corporation as the legal owner of shares of the share capital of a public or private corporation. Shareholders may be referred to as members of a corporation.

Short-term financial goal: A financial goal that will require less than six months to achieve.

Simple interest: This is calculated by multiplying the daily interest rate by the principal, then by the number of days that elapse between payments.

Subprime mortgage crisis: The sharp increase in high-risk mortgages that went into default beginning in 2007, contributing to the most severe recession in decades. The housing boom of the mid-2000s, combined with low-interest rates at the time, prompted many lenders to offer home loans to individuals with poor credit.

Tax exemption: A factor that reduces or eliminates a person's obligation to pay tax.

Tax lien: A lien imposed by law on a property to secure the payment of taxes. A tax lien may be imposed for delinquent taxes owed on real property or personal property or as a result of failure to pay income taxes or other taxes.

Tax return: A tax form to be filed with a government body to declare liability for taxation.

Tax-deferred growth: Growth for which income taxes on investment earnings are not payable until the money is withdrawn.

Title insurance: A form of indemnity insurance that protects lenders and homebuyers from financial loss sustained from defects in a title to a property.

Valuation: An estimation of something's worth, especially one carried out by a professional appraiser.

Variable expenses: Expenses that change in price and frequency each month.

Variable interest rate: An interest rate that fluctuates based on market changes.

Vetting: The process of performing a background check on someone before offering them employment or conferring an award, which includes fact checking prior to making any decision. In addition, in intelligence gathering, assets are vetted to determine their usefulness.

Wholesaling: When a wholesaler contracts a home with a seller, then finds an interested party to buy it. The wholesaler contracts the home with a buyer at a higher price than with the seller and keeps the difference as profit.

This book has been inspired by Augie Byllott.

The motivation for this book is to bridge the gap between the future private moneylender to the inspiring investor.

CASE STUDIES

Chad Harris
Kenny LeBlanc
Jeff Cichocki
CJ Estel
Brighton Godwin
Al Williamson
Patrick Grayson
Jared Benjamin
Liz Poteet
Shawn McVicker
Greg Meech
Mr & Mrs Kurt Phillips
JJ Grits
Andy Grieb

THANK YOU'S

Walter Jenkins
John Day
Zach Lorenzen
Roger Godwin
Andrew Cross
Scooter Howell
Lee Haskins
Randy Vaillancourt
David Torres
Michael McClure
Crystal Caruthers
Russell Hunt
Jason Grotelueschen
Dawn Brooks
Keith Allen
Andrew Terrell
Brian Long
Will Blake
Damon Hammons
Chad Missildine
Rose Taylor
Misti Hudson
Lukas Zupan
Mike Todd
Dana Brown
Harrison Barbarick

About the Authors

Steven VanCauwenbergh is a long-time investor in income-producing properties. He has mastered the critical areas of purchasing, financing, renovating and managing real estate. He has authored several books and courses empowering people to reach their goals of financial freedom.

Builder of businesses would be an accurate way to classify what Steven passionately does in multiple branches of economic disciplines including real estate, education, and the financial sector. Whenever he's not securing funding for investments, you'll find him on a trail riding his mountain bike.

Putting God first, family second, and business at a strong third.

Walter B. Jenkins, a professional writer/ghostwriter who is passionate about writing books, biographies, memoirs, and screenplays. It's not just his job. It's his calling.

Walter was an attorney and sports agent for ten years before becoming a full-time writer and speaker. He has a BA in English as well as a Juris Doctor and served as the Managing Editor of the Oklahoma City University Law Review.

SAVVY INVESTORS.COM

ADVANCED INVESTOR ALLIANCE PODCAST

AdvancedInvestorAlliance.com

SAVVY PODCAST

SavvyPodcast.com

Made in the USA
Monee, IL
04 November 2026

67382862R10095